VE DAY

A Day to Remember

VE DAY

A Day to Remember

by

Craig Cabell
and Allan Richards

Pen & Sword
MILITARY

First published in Great Britain in 2005 by
Pen & Sword Military
an imprint of
Pen & Sword Books Ltd
47 Church Street
Barnsley
South Yorkshire
S70 2AS

ISBN 1 84415 184 0

A CIP catalogue record for this book is
available from the British Library

Typeset in 11/13 Sabon by
Phoenix Typesetting, Auldgirth, Dumfriesshire

Printed and bound in England by
CPI UK

Pen & Sword Books Ltd incorporates the Imprints of Pen & Sword
Aviation, Pen & Sword Maritime, Pen & Sword Military, Wharncliffe
Local History, Pen & Sword Select, Pen & Sword Military Classics and
Leo Cooper.

For a complete list of Pen & Sword titles please contact
PEN & SWORD BOOKS LIMITED
47 Church Street, Barnsley, South Yorkshire, S70 2AS, England
E-mail: enquiries@pen-and-sword.co.uk
Website: www.pen-and-sword.co.uk

Contents

Acknowledgements

We would like to thank the following for their time, reference and support:

The Imperial War Museum, the Air Historical Branch, the British Legion, the Douglas Bader Foundation (especially Lady Bader and Keith Delderfield), Gladys Stewart of the Women's Royal Army Corp Association, the National Archives at Kew. Charles Carter of the Royal British Legion, Major Rodger Bain of the Armed Forces Careers Office, and Leroy Gittens of the West Indies Ex-Servicemen's Association and Past Present Association The London Buffs.

Our heartfelt thanks are also due to: Simon Wiesenthal, Lord Janner of Braunstone, Sir Edward Heath, Frederick Forsyth, David L. Robbins, Raymond Baxter, John 'Cats Eyes' Cunningham, Dennis 'Hurricane' David, Angus Lennie and Ingrid Pitt.

Thanks are due to Shirley and Colin, Jean and Bernard, Anita, Samantha, Nathan and Fern, Mavis and Ian, Berny and Dave.

We would also like to thank the people who have contributed their memories to this book, some of whose stories have, unfortunately, had to be edited out. They are, in alphabetical order: Mabel (May) Violet Abbott, Florence Adams, Laura Adams, Rita Allen, Jack Baker, Marjorie Balcomba, John Banfield, Harold (Batch) Batchelder, James Bause, Gwen Borroff, Joyce Boulton, Molly

Bradley, Lena Branch, Harry Brimble, Joy Bruce, Alan Brundish, Daphne Brundish, John Campbell, Marjorie Carmichael, Helen Carter, Patricia Carvell, Barbara Chatten, Michoalina Cichowicz, Ron Clayton, Margaret Cormack, Mavis Dow, Brian Eccleshall, William Edmonds, Nora Fallon, Mary Foreman, Doris Gaines, Florence Sarah Gatling, Matthew Gibb, Arthur Goodsell, Iris Grace Gorder, Austen Green, Beryl Green, Jean Hall, Peter Harding, Evelyn Harper, Ivor Harris, Margaret Harris, Elizabeth Hays, Kenneth Peter Herterich, Edward Huzzey, Kay Jennings, Edna Jones, Alf Kennedy, Edward Kindler, Geoff Kirk, Alice (Cato) Catherina Allison-Krafft, Winifred Lankford, Elsie Law, Bernard Ledwidge, Bill Lindsey, Cora Lovett, Evelyn Lucas, Alan Luckett, Margaret Luckett, Geoff Luvick, Marie (Molly) Marfleet, James (Jim) Mariner, Iris Marshall, Neville Marshall, Phillis McGinnis, Mary McKeown, Ruth O'Connell, Irena Palmi, Mima Pannett, Owen Pannett, Henry Parker, Barbara Pettyfer, George Phillips, May Phillips, Norman Phillips, Bill Pinder, Eliane Plumer, Doris Porter, John Porter, Simone Porter, Sheila Puckle, Lilly Pye, Dora Rogers, Joan Rutland, Ron Seabrook, Marjorie Seelig, John Shilcock, Iris Smith, Margaret Smith, Roy Smith, Iris Spiers, Ruth Sproncz, Enid Stone, Betty Strickland, Thea Stride, Edward Szczepanik, Pelangie Throjanowska, Helen Thwaites, Jack Vaughan, May Vine, Norman Walls, David Wilson, Norman Wisdom, Evelyn Witt and Richard Yates.

In addition to those individuals who have contributed their memories, we would also like to express thanks to the staff at some residential homes. These include Elaine Ferris and the staff of Sunrise Assisted Living for efforts in organizing people to interview; Philomena Winterboer and the staff at Sheila Stead Home; Cheryl Fincham, Amelia Prodromou and the staff at Ashdene Home; Melanie Stewart and the staff at Ashglade Home; Alina Gaskin and the staff at the Antokol Polish Home and Kim Thomas, Chris Wisemen and the staff at the Nettlestead Home.

Sincerely, many thanks to you all.

Craig Cabell and Allan Richards
London, November 2004

Foreword

A Day to Remember by Frederick Forsyth

Even to say one recalls VE Day – 8 May 1945 – is a giveaway in the age department. One has to be over sixty!

Well, I remember it with great clarity. I was six years old, three months short of my seventh birthday in August. I was playing alone in my playroom at the top of the family house in Elwick Road, Ashford, Kent. It had seemed a spring day like any other: school, lessons, the bike ride home, the solitary wait until tea.

Then my mother was in the doorway, tears streaming down her face. The news of what had happened on Lüneberg Heath that morning had just come through on 'the wireless'.

Being too young to understand, I thought tears in a grown-up (as in a child) indicated pain and anguish. The idea of anyone crying from relief or joy was not within my understanding. So I just stared dumbly, a wooden Spitfire in my hand.

Then she ran across the floor, dropped to her knees, wrapped her arms round me and kept repeating: 'It's over, it's over'.

When you are six, being embraced by a blubbing Mum who starts talking nonsense is pretty unsettling stuff. What was over? Tea? I had not even had it. Then she increased the vocabulary. 'The war is over,' she said. That made sense.

I took it pretty calmly. I could not recall a day when there was not a war. It started when I was thirteen months old – before the onset of memory. And for me it was not all bad, not by a long chalk.

It meant a limitless collection of bits of shrapnel, shiny .303 brass cases collected from the fields where they fell after being ejected from fighters overhead.

It meant being made a fuss of by the Polish soldiers manning the ack-ack battery on the waste ground across the road, without understanding that they had left small children behind in Warsaw to come and fight far away.

It meant priceless fragments of German equipment brought back from Europe by returning Tommies – a belt buckle with *Gott Mit Uns* stamped on it; even a German shoulder flash. A chap could be a big hit at school with things like that.

It meant being able to march up and down the playground singing 'Hitler has only got one ball, Goebbels has two but very small . . .' to the tune of Colonel Bogey, until the turkey-purple Miss Stock came running out to silence such language.

It meant the Odeon on Saturday morning with the Movietone Newsreel showing heroic scenes of men charging and tanks roaring through the Rhine mud as we all cheered while waiting for the Lone Ranger to come after the news.

There were the downsides. It meant rationed food and sweets – but as I never knew them un-rationed, there was no contrast. It meant blocking all windows so that not a chink of light emerged after dark, although not a manned German bomber but only doodlebugs had been seen for months.

But as Mum held me and cried with relief and the end of five years' of pent-up tension, I thought that on balance winning the war was a good thing. It meant Dad would come home, hang up the khaki uniform for ever and never go away again.

There was no television back then, so we could not see the scenes of wild jubilation that swept over London. Not until the Movietone newsreel a week later would we see the massed crowds swamping Trafalgar Square, or 'Winnie' beaming from the balcony of Buckingham Palace flanked by the King, Queen and two princesses.

Down in Ashford, as in every township and village in the country, people ran up to strangers to exchange the news, and the church bells rang on and on.

There would be more news, not all good. The awful pictures

from Bergen-Belsen camp, the first to be liberated by our Tommies; the end of the war against Japan with the dropping of two bombs that a small boy could simply not begin to imagine; the pictures of our own POWs released as skeletons from Burma and Changi. The rage and the hatred would not diminish but grow; the triumph would be muted by images of a Europe in rubble, and then the Cold War, with its nuclear shadow for most of the rest of our lives.

But that sunny day in May 1945 was an innocent day. A day to remember.

Frederick Forsyth
February 2004

Introduction

'As the world early today awaited official news of the final German capitulation, unconfirmed reports said the Nazi commander in Norway, General Boehme, had offered to surrender.'

Sunday Express, 6 May 1945

This book marks the sixtieth anniversary of the end of the Second World War. For British civilians alive at that time, Victory in Europe (VE) Day, 8 May 1945, was a day to celebrate. However, for many civilians in Europe and other countries around the globe, it wasn't. For them, the pain continued.

VE Day should be a day of reflection and celebration. It is a day to remember and the sixtieth anniversary is important. It is a day which should remind us of the depths to which human beings can stoop. It should stand as a watchword against evil and, while they still live, it should be a celebration for war veterans the world over. Surely we must continue to acknowledge their courage and thank them, and their long dead comrades, for all that they achieved.

The human race must always be reminded of the suffering inflicted in the two world wars of the twentieth century. The veterans will die, but the consequences of such carnage have shaped the world we live in, for better or worse.

Before we analyse the momentous occasion that became VE Day, let us first examine the preceding events and what it was that made that particular time so important.

1

The surrender of all German forces did not happen on the same day and it certainly did not happen easily. They fought long and hard, prolonging the conflict. But inevitably, the end came. German armed forces in different areas of the conquered territories found they had little choice but to surrender as they became overwhelmed. The Germans had once been so powerful that it seemed as if nothing could stand in their way. But as the events rolled on through the end of April and into the beginning of May 1945, it was found that the same force that had conquered half of Europe had run out of steam. The troops were outnumbered and outgunned by fresh armies that poured in from what seemed to be all sides. The problem now was not so much whether to surrender but to which army; that from the west or from the east.

The final days of the European Second World War were turbulent times in Berlin. Adolf Hitler had gone into hiding within his bunker, located deep beneath the German Chancellery. There, surrounded by many of his senior officials, he consistently refused to accept that utter defeat was about to befall his once grand empire. He had conceived a dream of a federated Europe; federated under his ultimate control and he obviously had no intention of letting that slip away. He had fought in the Great War. He had subsequently witnessed the demolition of Germany, largely – though not entirely – by the Allied countries of Britain, France and America. The war guilt and reparations imposed after that war, had placed a terrible and crushing burden on Germany. Unemployment had been massive. Inflation was so rife that there were stories of people being paid with cash in wheelbarrows and rushing to the shops before the wheelbarrows became worth more than the cash they carried. Within this horror, Hitler had witnessed the poverty that followed. He believed that the Jews were immune to the struggle everyone else was enduring. He rose to great heights in Germany with promises of economic stability and great power and he dragged the nation, and indeed much of the world, through another huge conflict to rival the one in which he had previously fought.

By the spring of 1945, the German Empire – the Third Reich – was crumbling. It had once encompassed approximately half of the European landmass. But even the area that became known as

Greater Germany, which engulfed Austria and much of Poland, was under serious threat. As the final days approached, Allied troops used a combination of military power and weight of numbers to liberate vast areas of the European mainland almost as swiftly as those same areas had been conquered less than a decade before. The Allies suffered setbacks too, like the disastrous campaign for a bridge in northern Europe, made famous by the film *A Bridge Too Far*. But on the whole, it was the military strength of the Allies that would prevail.

Hitler, hiding in his underground bunker, issued a set of orders to his people. Those between the ages of sixteen and sixty were ordered to fight. Everyone who could must fight to defeat the invaders. If the invasion continued and became unstoppable, then everything must be destroyed. He planned a scorched earth policy as a last resort. The Allies would inherit a wasteland. There would be nothing left. He may have had little idea that much of his empire had fallen already. Ironically, General Siegfried Henrici, the officer tasked with carrying out the scorched earth policy, did not actually need to see it through. The Allies, and particularly the Russians, were doing a fine job of destroying Germany themselves.

Most empires are built on suppression and violence, and most fade in the same way, often faster than they are built. The empire that had been Hitler's dream seemed to be no exception.

Goering, the chief of the German air force and one of those closest to Hitler, saw himself as the natural successor to the Führer. He had served alongside Hitler for several years and had been loyal and trustworthy. He was a logical choice, even if he, himself, had made that decision. Hitler however, viewed this as treason and ordered that his comrade be arrested. Perhaps it was a punishment, perhaps a deterrent to others, or perhaps Hitler was just panicking.

His personal secretary, Martin Bormann, had enjoyed special access to the Führer and virtually controlled his flow of information. If part of the reason for Hitler's apparent stubbornness in the face of such overwhelming collapse was a lack of information, then surely some of the blame must rest at the feet of Bormann.

Among his other important duties, he had the unenviable task of arranging the final execution authorized by Hitler – that of SS

Lieutenant General Hermann Fegelein. Fegelein, the brother-in-law of Hitler's mistress, Eva Braun, had dared slip out of the bunker. When he was recaptured, he was stripped of his rank and executed.

One of the most momentous events during the entire war was the death of Adolf Hitler. He finally realized that all hope of salvaging his empire was in ruins. He sent his personal staff, including Bormann, into the corridor outside his bunker room. Hitler and Eva Braun were left alone. A few moments later, the staff heard a single shot. When they re-entered, they found the Führer dead. He had shot himself in the mouth. Eva Braun had swallowed poison. Their bodies were transported to the courtyard and, in obedience to their final wishes, were soaked in petrol and burned.

Hitler's Propaganda Minister, Josef Goebbels, who had also been present that day, made an attempt the following day to arrange a truce between Germany and the Allied Expeditionary Force. This failed and he followed his superior through the suicide option, but not before he had arranged the murders of his six children and his wife.

Few high-ranking officials remained in the German High Command. One who was left was General Karl Weidling, the Military Commandant of Berlin. It was left to him to organize the unconditional surrender of all German forces. But before that, he had the dubious task of informing what remained of the military that their leader was dead.

The influential departures and suicides continued. General Krebs killed himself, as did the euthanasia mastermind Professor Max de Crinis. Bormann attempted to escape but probably did not reach any safe area. There were no safe areas left. The Russians controlled Berlin. Their flag flew over the Reichstag.

Another departure, although not from Berlin, was Dr Ante Pavelic. He was one of Hitler's closest allies and the ruler of Croatia. He issued an instruction from his base in Zagreb – 'If we must die, let us fall as true heroes, not as cowards crying for mercy'. Then he fled north to Austria and on to the relative safety of Argentina.

The end in sight, the signing of the actual surrender document seemed almost a formality. But it was an important formality; so important it actually took two attempts.

At 3 p.m. on 8 May 1945, the announcement was made across a relieved and joyful British nation that the day would be treated as Victory in Europe (VE) Day and would, therefore, be regarded as a holiday. The following day would also be a holiday.

Although the war against Japan continued, for those in Britain on 8 May 1945, there was no doubt that they had reached a tremendously powerful and memorable day in the history of the twentieth century. People from the occupied territories were free of the stamp of jackboots; those nightmarish days when armed troops rampaged through their houses and took whatever they wanted.

So what then of VE Day sixty years on? It is a long time to commemorate one particular day. Life does go on and we have to ask ourselves, 'Why should we remember that period all these years later? Why should people who were not even alive then be told?' The answer is simple: it is because of the exploits of millions of people, both military and civilian, who gave their lives for freedom not totalitarianism.

In our lives today we take much for granted: our freedom to determine our own destinies and our knowledge that we won't be dragged from our homes and subjected to humiliating torture. We take for granted our ability to purchase foods and other items without resorting to ration cards or overpriced black market supplies. There are no curfews. There are no public executions as retaliation for military deaths, or because an officer feels in the mood to kill a few randomly selected people. We are able to speak out against government policies without the terror of being dispatched immediately to death camps where gas or bullet means a fate swifter than starvation. We enjoy the freedoms we have partly because of the way the Second World War in Europe ended. It could have been so very different. VE Day should always be remembered, not just for those who toiled to make it happen, but for those of us alive and free today because it did happen.

When discussing VE Day, it is necessary to draw upon infor-mation from more than just one day. The events of those few days at the end of April and the beginning of May 1945 were momentous. They shaped the world in which we lived for the next fifty years and, to some extent, still live in today.

The separation of East and West Germany, for example, was a direct result of the territories claimed by the Allied Expeditionary Force in the west and the Russian Army in the east. The Berlin Wall and the Cold War itself, all came from what happened on the days surrounding that one event sixty years ago. These are all additional reasons to remember VE Day.

This isn't a book simply marking celebration; it is a book that recognizes the horror of the Second World War also. We respectfully dedicate it to all those who fought and lived, and to all those who died that we might live in peace.

Chapter One

The Civilian Impact on VE Day

'It was a high old time in Trafalgar Square last night. Everybody wanted to climb something. This party of Wrens and Allied soldiers celebrated by clambering on to the lions. Army policemen present – like Nelson on his column – turned a blind eye.'

Daily Mirror – Tuesday, 8 May 1945

While the armed forces of the Allied nations completed an outstanding task to bring about VE Day, it is often the civilians working in support that are forgotten. Yet, for the bulk of them, VE Day brought with it a unique opportunity to celebrate. The military were, largely, still overseas, trying to maintain and enforce the surrender. There were some civilians alongside them, primarily in the roles of logistics and medical staff. But the vast majority of the non-military population was at home and each person was able to celebrate VE Day in his or her own way. They celebrated as much as their personal circumstances allowed. In some cases, they chose not to celebrate at all. But whatever they did, it is important to remember that there was at least something to celebrate. Each of them played their own vital role in turning that dream into a reality.

Traditionally, wars prior to the Second World War had taken heavy tolls on the military forces fighting to safeguard their respective nations. Whether those military forces were composed of civilians who volunteered to fight or regular soldiers who were compelled to fight, each individual learnt very quickly, sometimes painfully, that the job came with some element of risk. In fact, if counting just military casualties, the Great War was the largest killer in history.

The Second World War changed the scenario. Suddenly, the conflict was taken to a new level. It was fought over many areas and virtually everyone, including civilians, was directly involved. Air power was growing and nations like Great Britain, which previously had been spared total and direct involvement in its own territory, suddenly found itself as much in the front line as any other. Homes were no longer safe as bombing raids created huge waves of destruction in heavily populated cities.

What was desperately needed was the full input of the civilian population, most of whom had neither the ambition nor the experience to fight a successful conflict. What those people could do however, and by all accounts did remarkably well, was support from the background. Under constant threat of bombardment, they toiled in their respective roles. Often, those roles were decided for them rather than by them. They built the munitions their military comrades used, to devastating effect, in trying to beat the enemy into submission. The factories were, quite logically, prime targets and any direct hit on a factory dedicated to the construction of bombs would almost certainly destroy the entire complex and everyone within.

Mining was one role that Britain depended upon. Starved of foreign supplies, yet desperate for fuel to keep people warm in winter and to keep factories running, coal was a commodity that, thankfully, Britain had in reasonable supply. All that was needed was the manpower to extract it. That was where people like Kenneth Peter Herterich came in:

Working down in the coal mines was very, very hard work. We worked long shifts, usually eight hours at a time, with no lunch break. We ate our sandwiches while at the coalface. I was a Bevin Boy, so called after Ernest Bevin, the minister who devised the scheme for recruiting miners into the army. There was then plenty of scope for the likes of me to go into the mines. Each person had a specific task. There were the drillers – they drilled the holes for the explosives, then there were the blasters, who obviously handled that side of the process, then the fillers scooped the coal and removed it from the mine.

I was looking after the pit ponies, animals destined to spend their lives down in the mines. I also operated the railway. The rails were an efficient method of transporting large amounts of heavy coal from the coalface and out of the mine. The first mine I worked in was Stanley Pit in Durham, or rather under Durham. The next was New Biggin on Sea, near Blyth. The actual coalface for this one was one mile down and two miles out under the sea.

It was always very dangerous and difficult work, requiring a huge amount of manual strength and stamina. But everyone had a task to play in helping to win the war, and that was mine.

Towards the end of the war, I contracted meningitis and had to leave the mines. I had worked there for about two years by then and the departure meant that I was able to recover from the illness. When we all heard that the conflict had ended in Europe and we were able to celebrate VE Day, there was a tremendous party atmosphere. There were children out playing in the street; parents arranged trestles along some of the streets so we could have street parties. Of course, food was scarce then but we were determined that wasn't going to stop us having a damn good time.

Everyone went berserk, but it was all very well controlled by each person's sense of morality and goodwill to their neighbours. There were a lot of instances where people were strolling around, popping into each others' houses, making use of the open invitation that seemed to be part and parcel of that terrific day. I don't recall any social problems like you would have today. You wouldn't dream these days of opening your house to people walking past. You might loose half your possessions, or worse. But at that time, it just seemed so normal.

Other people could work in the fields, growing food to keep the people, both civilian and military, as well fed as possible.

Elizabeth Hays worked in the Land Army during the Second

9

World War. She worked in Scotland. She was twenty-four years old when the war ended. She explains her job for the Land Army and how she later heard that the war was over:

I started work for the Land Army in Aberdeenshire before moving on to Jedburgh, located in the border. There, I was on an estate owned by a Duke and the farm work was basically a bit of everything. Like many farms, there was a lot of diversification. The little fact that I am left handed actually came in quite useful because I could fill the carts from the other side to everyone else, so increase the workload that we could produce as a team. And teamwork was what a lot of the work was all about.

It's worth pointing out that I had absolutely no idea what I was doing. Before the war, I had not worked on a farm and I felt quite stranded. I had come from the city and worked in an office as a shorthand typist. I had absolutely no idea what to do with the crops I was supposed to be working with. I had to find turnips, sometimes under frozen ground and trample straw with an indoor thresher machine that didn't seem to care whether you slowed down. If you did, you got covered in straw. Those were just some of the new activities I had to come to terms with. But you learn fast – you have to when there's a war on.

There were quite a lot of differences in the privileges enjoyed by different people. For example, the landowner ate what we would term proper food, or at least proper food for the time, whilst we had food such as burnt semolina. I wasn't too fond of burnt semolina but when you're hungry your taste buds tend to get relegated to second place.

There were prisoners nearby. They were mostly Italian who seemed absolutely terrified of working in the rain. I rarely saw any guards monitoring them, although I suppose there must have been. There was plenty of contact between the prisoners and the local population – so much so that, after the war, three prisoners remained to marry local girls.

I had sciatica and that didn't do my Land Army role any favours. I ended my service in that organization and by the end of the war, I was back in the office I had been working in before. The firm's name was Buck & Hickman and it made anything from nails to milling machines. It had paid half my salary to my mother while I had been away doing my bit.

On VE Day itself, when the announcement came, I was in a theatre. I was with my family, including my sister and a wounded American cousin. We were watching *Lilac Time* starring Evelyn Laye. During the show, the announcement we had all been so desperate to hear came through. There was a huge uproar through the audience and to be perfectly honest, no one was really interested in the show after that. The rest of that particular performance was cancelled but I don't care that we didn't see the end. What we had heard was far more valuable than any play could possibly be.

There was this huge wave of relief and overjoyed emotion. Our people wouldn't be killed in Europe anymore. There was peace. Although Scotland wasn't so seriously rationed as England, we still had our shortages and now, finally, that too could change.

Later, I recall meeting someone on a train who met their husband actually at Trafalgar Square on VE Day. How's that for a wonderfully happy ending?

These Land Army memories of VE Day appear slightly romantic. Other memories, this time from England, come from Mary McKeown who was born in 1914 and was living in Cheshire during the Second World War:

I was involved in doing a bit of everything. One of the jobs was milking. I used to go around testing the quality of the milk, making sure it was drinkable or could be turned successfully into cheese. Milk was actually quite scarce because it had a limited shelf life. There wasn't much in the way of refrigeration, so unlike some other drinks, milk only lasted a day or so. Even turning it into cheese had to be done quickly, but then at least it would last longer. The other produce of the farm was mainly pigs and poultry. There was some breeding going on, purely for food purposes because,

11

of course, no one knew how long the war was going to last.

The farm had always been my home. I was always up early in the morning and exhausted by the evening, which unfortunately didn't allow much opportunity for socializing. And farming rarely left time for that anyway. I had been working on the family farm all the time, with my father, mother and brother. So unlike a lot of people, I saw my family all the time. Being lodged with the family the whole time and being so busy for long hours on the farm meant that, after a while, I was keen to get away for a little while. Perhaps when the war ended, I might be able to do that.

The regional headquarters of the Land Army in Cheshire was at Chumley Castle. A lot was coordinated from there. And it was also used as a sort of hospital for convalescence of patients, mainly sailors, who had been injured in the war. I did some nursing work too, in addition to my farming duties. That was how we got through the war. Everyone did what they could, and as much as they could.

When VE Day arrived, I was at the Castle. I remember being there when the announcement was made and that was where we all celebrated. We didn't overdo it. It wasn't necessary. There was still a lot to accomplish and a lot to wonder about. But we had a glass of wine each and felt we finally had the freedom to talk about the past few years. But we were also wondering what was going to happen to the Land Army as a whole. Did the end of the war mean the end of the Land Army?

Some of us, very naively, expected everything to return to normal overnight. We would, they supposed, all be disbanded very quickly and the country would rapidly return to normal. But of course, that's not how it happened and the less optimistic, more realistic of us realized that it would take quite some time.

We were also wondering about what we would do as a nation with all the extra people who had been fighting and now no longer were. How could places be found for them? They had been fighting for so long, what were they going to do now? With the war still raging against Japan perhaps some soldiers might be sent there.

I couldn't believe that the war had finally finished in Europe. The conflict had mapped out a timetable for me for the past five years, working between the castle and the farm. Suddenly, that stopped and I could map out my own timetable, relinquishing the work at the castle. I could go back to being a farmer's daughter.

Relationships would also be easier to develop. Men were coming back from the war and because my time at the castle had ceased, I had a little more time to myself. It was very nice.

As far as food was concerned during the war, a large proportion of it came from overseas. With almost strangling blockades, there had to be an alternative. Thousands who had never even picked up a trowel suddenly found themselves doing their part to feed a country that would otherwise have been starved into submission. They had to make the best of a bad job working to produce crops that would grow in the British climate.

Gwen Boroff, a teacher during the war, gives an account of how it became frighteningly normal to lose a student.

> The bulk of my time was spent teaching others. There had been one girl at college who suddenly wasn't there the next day. When I asked where she was – the house had been bombed that night and the whole family had been wiped out. That was tragic and it sent a shiver through us all. Yet it was so normal; perhaps the normality was just as tragic.
>
> I remember a bomb explosion in Lewisham, which is near where I lived in Catford. I was blown through Burton's window in the High Street – one way of getting into the shop! It was a large explosion and my coat must have got caught on the way in because it was torn and not from the mass of smashed glass all over me.
>
> I used to have a short train journey each day and it was always terrifying. If you heard a hissing noise, everyone hunched forwards and braced themselves. It would usually be a bomb coming down. The Germans targeted that particular line quite a lot because of all the troop movement

in the area, with the soldiers crammed in and leaning out of the windows. They made a nice target for the enemy.

On VE Day, I think everyone celebrated in their own way. Schools and colleges were closed for the day. My father threw the house open, so to speak, and neighbours just flowed in. That was quite a popular thing to do. There wasn't much time for preparations so everything had to be pretty impromptu. All the doors were open and everyone just congregated around whichever door was open. The spirits were so high and we had a fine time. I think there were even some people who perhaps couldn't get wine, celebrating with a glass of water and pretending. It all went on until the early hours of the morning. It was typical, I think, of the Englishman. They all loved to celebrate something.

It was a day of relief. It was the end of a war where civilians were almost as likely to be killed as the military. The service personnel, when they sign up, accept some risk, but suddenly, with this war, the danger was brought into the lives of civilians too. The end meant that we could finally go about our lives; we could finally travel to work in peace, not in pieces.

From that day, we could start thinking about the simple things to entertain ourselves. For instance, there were very few cinemas and theatres open. And you always had to make a decision during the war. Would you go to see a play and risk a direct hit from a bomb?

Suddenly, saying hello to someone seemed different. We knew that we would probably all be alive the next morning. Previously, that wasn't the case. Before, you could be talking to someone on the train and the next day you might not see him. 'Where is he?' 'He got a direct hit last night.' It would all have been as casual as that. 'That's a shame.' What could you do? VE Day changed all that.

I think the younger generation think about it, but they didn't have our spirit of relief, the cloud of war was gone. Students nowadays talk about pressure but I think the pressure was higher during the war. You had to pass everything because there may not be a second chance. Studying was harder then than now because you had the added problem of trying to study with constant air raids. I don't think much is written about that. It was hard work and they had a really rough deal.

Mother would send them off to school in the morning, never knowing whether she would see them again, kids never knowing whether they would see their home and parents again every day. And on top of that, they had to study and take exams and go home and complete their homework, always knowing they might be interrupted and have to find shelter from the bombs. Once you hear a bomb falling, it's a sound you never forget.

It was a world where attachments to other people and indeed relationships were difficult to establish, especially with so many people fighting overseas; a world where invasion by hostile forces was a possibility, and for many in Europe a reality; a world where the young had never known anything other than bombs and fighting.

It is easy to look back in hindsight and say 'well we won' and take that for granted, but at the time victory was not so clear cut. For example, if we look at the work novelist Dennis Wheatley did for the Joint Planning Staff (JPS) of the War Cabinet, we can clearly see through his papers the desperation at trying to activate the civilian on homeland security. The Government was convinced that the Germans would attempt to invade the UK and they were not far wrong. Operation Sea Lion had been planned and could have been pulled off. However Wheatley had pre-empted the Germans' plan, as he wrote in *Stranger Than Fiction*:

> . . . after the war, we secured copies of Operation Sea Lion – the real German plan of invasion. They intended to use all the airborne forces they could muster on Kent, but I may perhaps be pardoned for my delight when, all those years later, I learned that I had been proved right in my major assumption; that it was upon our south-east coast that they meant to launch their all-out assault.

Wheatley would write his plans throughout the night. He didn't believe that there was a moment to lose. He stated on more than one occasion that in one forty-eight hour period, without sleep, he drank several magnums of champagne and wrote 30,000 words' worth of war plans.

So VE Day brought with it a great sense of relief. British civilians could learn to relax a little more, content in the knowledge that the Nazi threat had been quashed. Different people decided to celebrate in different ways. Nothing formal had been organized and people seemed to make the best of what they had but no one wanted to miss out on the celebrations or, more to the point, allow their children to miss out. David Bush, a young boy during the Second World War explained:

> We lived in Charlton, south-east London, and were evacuated the day after a V2 rocket blew up Charlton railway station.
> I was taken to Oxford. I stayed at the college and punted on the river, but although I had a good time, it wasn't so good for my mother who had to work hard whilst away.
> It was while in Oxford, that I heard of the victory in Europe. A man was riding along on his bicycle and telling everyone who would listen that the war was over. It didn't mean much to me, apart from the fact that I'd probably get more sweets now.
> When we eventually came home, a VE party was held for us children up on Charlton heights, so we didn't miss out on the celebrations!

Sometimes life – evacuation – was a new adventure for the children, but for the adults it was a different story. Evacuation was not always sweetness and light, as we shall hear from Daphne Brundish. She was a child when the war began, living in the East End of London. One of her most vivid memories of that early period was the collective unity of neighbours helping each other dig into gardens to construct the Anderson shelters for the inevitable bombing.

> You had to bury the shelters down into the ground and then cover the roof with soil. My parents even put plants on the

top. We had five bunk beds, my parents together, then my younger sister and I together, then my even younger brother by himself at the end. My sister was a pain to get into the shelter. She didn't like getting up in the middle of the night so we had to drag her out. She was only about three. The raids became so frequent that we virtually lived in the shelter, even eating our meals in what became a second home. After the raids, we used to go out searching for shrapnel – souvenirs.

Then we got bombed out. When that happened, there was some mesh in the door and I can remember my father calling to me not to move. The mesh was right up against my throat and if I'd moved, I would have been killed instantly. The piano took a battering and it still bares the scars of flying debris. One of my school friends was killed when she and her family remained in the house when it was flattened.

As a family, excluding my father, we moved to live with my mother's cousin. We remained there for about six months. My father managed to get another house but had to have two children living there. So my mother, brother and sister returned, leaving me. I used to travel to school on the milk cart. My grandmother was living there and she was very strict. I was never allowed to be ill, even when I was suffering from ear infections. Apparently, I was lying about any illness.

I did manage to get home when my father was ill and my grandmother no longer wanted me with her. I remember one time when I was at school, we all had to stay behind once because there were a lot of jeeps and other military vehicles trundling past and we literally couldn't get out. This was towards the end of the war and I suppose it might have had something to do with troop movements in preparation for D-Day.

I have since read that the metal railings that were removed and all the pans and stuff that were taken to make guns and jeeps and aircraft was purely a PR exercise. That way, the public could be convinced it was doing its bit for the war effort. But none of it was ever used. I'm not sure how true that is.

I definitely remember the street party we had for VE Day.

My mother made aprons with Union Jacks for my sister and me. My brother had a hat he didn't want to wear. I recall it was constantly being removed by him and replaced by my mother. It was like a running battle. There was music – people playing different instruments. There were singsongs with the old 78 speed records and the wind-up players.

It certainly wasn't the end of rations. Even when I was going to work, there were still rations. Food had been cut and patted on a piece of paper to ensure the right amount. We did have a chicken dinner for Christmas, but only because we could get that from a relative. Bread was grey in colour and I think probably healthier than now because it didn't have the same sort of bleaches and additives in it. Eggs were still rationed, so was butter, meat, sweets and clothes. My sister always had the clothes I had grown out of because there was no other option. It had been something we had got used to for so long it had become the normal routine. Even the arrival of VE Day didn't alter that too much. It just meant improvements were then in sight.

People were also thinking of loved ones further away than Europe, still fighting and dying. But it wasn't all horror; even for some loved ones far away the war was over, as Norman Walls, a captain in the Royal Artillery, explained:

My first sight of a V1 rocket was when I was in Tilbury docks, preparing for D-Day. I had no idea what it was. It was coming in so low; people on towers were looking down on it. Later, once we learnt what those things were, we still had little hope of shooting them down so the Spitfires used to nudge their fins to try to flip them off course.

I didn't go across to Europe on D-Day. I went after. We worked our way through Belgium and Holland. My unit had troops strategically placed along the various routes so we knew where each mobile gun battery was at any time. I started with one of these drop off points and collated the information. That was all coded of course. I remember on one occasion, a unit needed a barge and crane to tackle a canal.

So the coded request came through for a hippopotamus and giraffe.

Towards the end, I was involved in the shell barrage across the River Rhine. By the time my unit reached the outskirts of Hamburg, we knew the war was virtually over. There was an abandoned house en route and we decided to shelter in it for the night. There was a radio inside. I listened to a German programme through this and that was how I heard that the German forces had surrendered.

On VE Day, I remember seeing someone going along the street, writing on the doors with a stick of chalk. He was writing different numbers – five – six – three – and so on. When he was asked what he was doing, he said he was writing how many troops each house could accommodate for the night. We drove around Hamburg quite happily, having a really good day and I remember receiving thanks from the unit, for all my help.

The above story illustrates the plight of one man during the war and the small amount of celebrations he had time to indulge in. Yes, his loved ones were concerned about him, but the war was over and he would be home soon. But what about the people whose war was far from over?

David Wilson was twenty-one at the end of the Second World War. The family home was in a small village called Peldon, near Colchester, and he attended boarding school in Weymouth, Dorset, until the end of 1940. He was the son of a parish rector.

He performed his role in the war effort serving in the Merchant Navy, primarily on the famous Atlantic convoys. His vital role managed to keep Britain fighting, bringing in desperately needed supplies, mainly of food and fuel. The Merchant fleets were often prime targets for German U-boats, tasked with sinking as much Allied shipping as possible.

He lost three years of his life while incarcerated in a prisoner of war camp. It was not a German camp but a Japanese one, from which the death rate of prisoners was five times higher than from their European counterparts. German guards were often viewed as being vicious and brutal but this paled in comparison with the harsh conditions inflicted upon the prisoners struggling to survive in a Japanese prisoner of war camp. Approximately twenty-four per cent of prisoners in Japanese POW camps died during those cruel years, compared with about five per cent from German POW camps.

No remembrance of VE Day would be complete without a serious study of the other side of the coin; without analysing the thoughts of people who, whilst those in Britain celebrated peace and salvation, were still suffering and dying at the hands of the Japanese. Here is David Wilson's story:

After I left school, I joined the Merchant Navy. That was in April 1941, when the Battle of the North Atlantic was at its most severe. For much of that year, the ship I was serving on was engaged in bringing desperately needed food and other supplies across from America. We sailed in convoys for as much protection as possible and the most dangerous threat came from below the surface. German U-boats were always operating in the area, each sinking as much shipping as possible, trying to starve Britain into submission.

In March 1942, we loaded up with munitions and other supplies in New York. Our destination was the Eighth Army in the Middle East. The engines of the ship were sabotaged before we left and we broke down off the coast. As the engineers were struggling to repair the damage, we actually saw five other merchant ships being torpedoed within sight and fully expected to be next. But we did manage to get moving again and escaped. Our next point of call was St Lucia. There was already a ship in the harbour. That vessel was struck by a torpedo from a U-boat, right there in the harbour. I think that if our engines had not been wrecked, that could have been me.

We were part of a convoy of five ships, heading for the Middle East around the Cape of Good Hope as the Mediterranean was closed to British shipping at that time. All five ships were on a secret route and all five ships were shelled by a German surface raider called *The Thor*.

After several other events, we eventually came ashore in

Yokohama and were incarcerated in a Japanese prisoner of war camp. I was in that dreadful place for the next three years. Abuse of prisoners was rife and seemed to be acceptable to the guards. We were virtually starved, brutally treated and constantly humiliated.

We were not allowed to take cover from attacking planes if they were fighter bombers. If they were heavy bombers, it depended on the time of day. If the attack was during the day, we could go under cover. If it was during the night – and towards the end of the war attacks happened almost every night – we were forced to stand in the middle of the road hoping, presumably that we would be hit. We made it a point of honour that, although we were absolutely terrified, we would stand to attention and show the guards up. They always scuttled to a shelter when the bombs fell too near.

My horrific life there for those torturous three years left me with a hatred of anything Japanese. That, to some extent has finally started to dwindle over the years that have followed, but I will always find it difficult to forget and forgive the loss of 12,433 young men from these shores who died in those prison camps.

VE Day presented a dilemma to us. On the one hand, we were pleased that the war in Europe was over because our families at home would now be much safer. But on the other hand, the news of no more fighting in Europe filled us with trepidation. We knew we were now likely to be on the receiving end of a far worse hammering than before. We had heard the news about halfway through May 1945, when the coolies we worked with (the lowest of the low in the eyes of the Japanese) managed to inform us of what was going on. As I said, our feelings about that were very mixed.

When I was finally released in August 1945, my body weight had plummeted to a painful six and a half stone. As the prisoners started returning home, the medical authorities did not know what to do with us and how to treat us, so they selected the 'Do Nothing' option. Many of us found it very difficult settling down to a normal life and some felt compelled to take their own lives or found themselves suffering divorce from wives who could not understand. It was years before we settled down again and some are still suffering.

VE Day meant very little because we were still incarcerated with little sight of any release. The whole Far East situation continued for another three months and now, I think, it is all but ignored, except by those connected in some way or with a genuine interest. I think there are some people who are bliss-fully unaware that Japan was even involved in the Second World War.

And I am also horrified that the Merchant Navy does not receive much acclaim for the essential and extremely dangerous role it performed. Seventeen per cent of merchant seamen lost their lives, along with about 2,600 ships. This sacrifice is often ignored. Everyone serving had volunteered and everyone at home received the benefit. The most dangerous cargo was fuel, essential for the military to continue the war effort and civilians to waste in their cars. When a tanker was hit, the crew could be roasted alive. How long would Britain have lasted without the efforts of the Merchant Navy?

So people were scattered over the world. Some had been liberated, some had been released from death camps; others were still incarcerated in them, some people had been released from the forces or were just civilians enjoying the freedom won.

Rita Allen was one such civilian who had a bird's eye view of the VE Day celebrations in London, and when her story is read in comparison with David Wilson's above, a balanced view of VE Day and what it meant then, can truly be pictured:

I can remember the first air raid warning very well. It must have been the first of the war since it came on the same day we heard the announcement. Thankfully, it was only a false warning, but we didn't know that at the time.

I was working in banking during the war. For me at least,

banking was a reserved occupation so I wasn't likely to get called up into the forces. The branch I worked in was at Pall Mall in London. There were a lot of air raid warnings all the time and, at the beginning, there was not really much of a structured system for dealing with the problem. Before the claxons, someone at the top of our building, seven floors up, could see a flag across the park. When that told him there was a possible attack, he would use string and tin cans to alert someone else, who would then use the same method and so on.

I lived with my mother and brother. My brother was also working in banking at the start of the war. Then he was called into service and joined the Royal Navy. He served mainly on minesweepers, helping to keep shipping lanes clear because the Germans were always laying mines. He and his crew, along with some of the other minesweepers, were the first across the channel on D-Day. The waterways had to be cleared otherwise the whole campaign wouldn't even have reached the beaches.

I was able to develop a relationship with my brother's friend, who I saw quite a lot through my brother. One thing led to another and we eventually got married. So, I suppose, had it not been for my brother's involvement in the Navy, and indeed the war itself, I never would have met my husband.

On VE Day, I was in the building where I had been working. I was glad to be there because it gave me a wonderful overview of the whole event. I had a sort of bird's eye view of the celebrations. I saw more than I would have if I had been down on the ground. The procession was terrific and the Mall was the best place to be. I was looking down on the Mall and all the people going by. I hadn't seen any processions during the war and I just loved it. I thought it was truly wonderful.

But for a lot of people, it was very much business as usual, so the time when the whole area became really totally crowded was when people could be on their lunch hours. Especially then, the atmosphere was very exciting, wonderfully exciting. I was so lucky to be on the top floor of the building because I had one of the best views. I didn't miss anything that I might have done otherwise.

It was an end to windows being blown out by bombs exploding. It was an end to barrage balloons floating overhead, although I think by VE Day, most of them had been removed anyway. It also meant an end to my other task in addition to the banking: I used to do fire watching during the war. There was a wonderful sense of relief that the war was over.

I remember on one occasion there was a little child with her mother on a tram. She was showing everyone her new shoes and was really proud of them. That night, a bomb dropped and she was gone. That kind of uncertainty had come to an end for us on VE Day. It was such a great feeling. And we wouldn't see any more of the flying bombs – the doodlebugs. They were really worrying because no one knew where any of them would land. I doubt whether the Germans even knew where they would go either.

During some air raids, my nephew had slept in a dresser drawer because that was quite a safe place for him and he was small enough to fit quite snugly. Of course, when the War finished and there would be no more air raids, such sleeping arrangements would no longer be necessary.

That special day also meant an end to seeing all the sandbags along the streets. They had been all over the place. You couldn't move for sandbags. There was also the problem of blackouts that could finally come to an end. Sometimes during those blackouts, if you were on a train and it pulled into a station, you had trouble getting off. You may not even see the station, and because the passengers opened all the doors, you could, and sometimes did, get off the train on the wrong side and fall onto the tracks heading the other way. That was especially a problem if you weren't familiar with the route and had no idea which side of the train the platform would be on.

There was a hugely tremendous feeling of excitement everywhere on VE Day. People were rushing around all over the place, looking for good vantage points for the celebrations and the parades. There had never been anything like it before.

All the above illustrates the broad range of emotions people were going through on VE Day the world over – either military or civilian. But how was victory achieved against what appeared to be insurmountable odds?

Chapter Two

Hitler vs Churchill

'A Germany without Adolf Hitler would not be fit to live in.'
Eva Braun, on her last journey from Munich to Berlin to join
Hitler in his bunker, 15 April 1945.

The death of Adolf Hitler cannot be underestimated in its importance. Whilst he was, undeniably, a disastrous military tactician, he did have a flair for theatricals that boosted the morale of a depressed nation and consequently propelled that nation to new heights.[1] Yet that flair ultimately took the country to the brink of absolute and crushing devastation such as it had not witnessed since the end of the Great War.

He came into power at a time when Germany was at the lowest point in its history. Germany had been blamed for all the losses in the Great War and was suffering disastrous economic deprivation. He was a dynamic speaker who was able to bring together a divided and collapsing nation. His warped ideas of purity of people and of what was and what wasn't acceptable only came to light later, long after his astoundingly successful rise to power.

Having served as a corporal in the army, his leadership experience was limited. Yet, despite that obvious disadvantage, obvious to everyone except he himself, he installed himself in a position of absolute power over those with greater skill and experience at planning warfare.

His failings created a great many disputes and a lot of unrest.

As events started to turn against Germany, Field Marshall Erwin Rommel met with some of the other leaders of the *Wehrmacht* to discuss how they could reach an armistice with the western Allies without Hitler's involvement. This occurred as early as May 1944, even before D-Day. In fact, Hitler became so despised by many of his generals that some plotted to assassinate him. The attempt, on 20 July 1944, of course failed, but it did have the effect of driving him further into the paranoid insanity that would eventually bring down the entire Third Reich.

Whether he knew whom he could trust was doubtful. His behaviour towards the end of April 1945 demonstrates that his mind was becoming even more illogical and paranoid. He was clear that his nation did not deserve to continue if everyone did not fight until they were dead. Surrender, in his mind, was not even an option. The Nazi party he had devised was, in his own personal utopia, supreme, and how could 'the supreme' surrender to someone inferior? Its doctrine utterly forbade even the consideration of either defeat or capitulation. He expected all his people – military and civilian, adults and children – to engage the enemy and create, if necessary, a guerrilla warfare situation in Berlin.

He refused to see reason. He refused to listen to his advisers if they dared utter anything about surrender or defeat, or even negotiation. He refused to accept that he might have been wrong in any of his decisions. In some ways, he was displaying a very Japanese style of thinking. The Japanese continued to fight and treated prisoners with appalling contempt because they saw surrender as a sign of weakness. It was dishonourable and worse than a glorious death. Hitler's view was clearly much the same towards the end of his life. In fact he felt that, if the German people were defeated, they had no entitlement to exist. The only alternative to victory was absolute annihilation.

Then finally, wishing to remain a Nazi to his dying breath, he killed himself. In that one act, he had denied the families of his millions of victims the opportunity of bringing him to trial. He had made the ultimate decision for them, at his own choosing and in his own time.[2]

The date was 30 April 1945 and the noose was closing around

the neck of his capital city. Berlin, which had once stood as a proud and defiant symbol of his power, was virtually a pile of rubble.

One eyewitness to this devastation was Ian Dow, an intelligence officer who said: 'Berlin was a mess. I was one of the first (British) there. But then again all Germany was the same. It had been heavily bombed – flattened.'

As Mr Dow soon found though, despite being destroyed, Nazis still lurked in the damaged buildings: 'I went into one building – I won't say which – and as I opened the door to an innocuous looking room, I saw a German officer reach inside a drawer and pull out a gun. It was either me or him. And on that occasion it was him.'

Death was a day-to-day job for front-line troops, sometimes happening so quickly and unexpectedly it took time to work out what had happened, as Mr Dow explained:

> I was talking to a friend, lighting a cigarette in the street. We were fairly close to each other and then suddenly there was a gush of wind. When I got my senses back I looked around for my friend but he had disappeared, all that was left was his smoking boots.
>
> A bomb had gone off nearby and my friend had been in its path, I was barely outside that destructive path.

Some things can never be pre-empted; others can, as Mr Dow continued:

> I remember taking my motorbike down a quiet piece of road. Very quiet. I stopped, became very nervous, then quickly turned around and at full throttle returned home; an avalanche of machine gun fire exploded behind me.

But this was the dying embers of a beaten Germany. The military received a message from General Weidling:

> On 30 April 1945, the Führer, to whom we had all sworn allegiance, forsook us by committing suicide. Faithful to the

Führer, you, soldiers of Germany, were prepared to continue the Battle of Berlin, although your ammunition was running out and the general situation made further resistance senseless. I now order all resistance to cease forthwith.
Weidling
Artillery General
Commandant, Berlin Defence Region.

However, the civilian public were given a different version. On 2 May, a Nazi newspaper carried the headline 'Heroic Death of the Führer'. The news proclaimed that Hitler had been killed while fighting against the oppressors. He had died at the head of his troops.

Many people were known to rejoice when the news reached their eager ears. And regardless of how the death had happened and was reported, it was a fact. Adolf Hitler, the genius of manipulation and terror but hopeless at almost everything else, was dead. Although, as we have already seen, he was not a good military strategist, he was an excellent political and morale boosting figurehead. He had managed to keep Germany fighting, partly by his outstanding presence. After news of his death became common knowledge, that fighting spirit disintegrated until just a few days later, there was only pocket resistance. The Third Reich, which had been planned for a thousand years, was dead after less than a decade. The Nazi Party, and all the hatred and fear on which it capitalized, was finished. Berlin and the rest of Germany would soon be divided.

But what of Winston Churchill who became one of the most famous prime ministers in the history of Britain? His indelible presence and his rousing speeches led the nation through so many devastating trials and inspired Britain to stand firm against the German war machine. Virtually everywhere he went, he was greeted with enthralled patriotism. It was this community spirit that held the country together and enabled it to stand, at times, alone. It enabled Britain to make an outstanding contribution to the eventual downfall of the enemy.

Britain could not have had a more charismatic leader during the Second World War. He rallied people around him without the need to beat obedience into them. Whilst there were people searching for leaks of information, there were no organizations dedicated to extinguishing by death any signs of insurrection as there were in Germany. He brought the nation together and was able to inspire people into volunteering for sometimes even the most hazardous and arduous tasks. Everyone, and especially Churchill, had one goal in sight – to keep the country free from the invasions that had been seen in other European countries.

Everyone had a role to play and Churchill seemed to generate much of the intensity that each person adopted. Among the civilian duties, there was the Land Army, Merchant Navy, coal miners, factory workers, teachers, police, medical staff and fire staff. There was even a network of people waiting to be called into action should an invasion actually take place. This list is far from exhaustive, but it does illustrate the complex nature of struggle through the years of the Second World War and the difficulty associated with rallying everyone together into one common purpose. That rallying became the personal responsibility of the Prime Minister.

Bombs dropped, fires burned, civilians suffered and died. They had become fair game and were no longer protected behind the shields created by their military counterparts. Cities, ports, factories, even rail lines and farms, became valid targets. Without knowing which of their friends and family would be dead very soon, they toiled in their vital roles. And through it all, Churchill managed to keep the country together, moving along in the same direction and capitalizing on the community spirit that was essential to victory. VE Day was a chance for some, at least, to let their hair down.

As with Hitler, Churchill managed to get the public firmly behind him and discount any opposition. But that is where the similarities ended. Whilst Hitler and his henchmen chose very harsh and often lethal methods of ensuring support, Churchill favoured the power of the words he spoke. Leading a nation that was virtually isolated, he roused people to a determination to fight and to struggle and survive together.

Then, there were the armed services. Although Churchill kept a tight rein on what was going on throughout the war effort, he differed from his counterpart in Germany by allowing his military leaders far more rope. They had the experience. They had a job to do and he allowed them to do it. As long as he was able to keep overall control, they had far more freedom than Hitler allowed his military leaders. And, aside from that, Churchill had far more leadership experience than Hitler.

Many historians and academics have claimed that VE Day should not have happened, certainly not in favour of the Allies. Germany should have won the Second World War. So what happened? There were a number of factors that brought the result Britain and many other countries so desperately needed – luck, military power in the right place at the right time, disastrous decisions on the part of the enemy but, most of all, the resolve of the British people.

It was fitting that on VE Day, Winston Churchill stood beside the Royal family on the balcony of Buckingham Palace and it was so like him to dedicate the victory to the public that had stood firm beside him.

In one of its darkest and most dangerous periods in history, Britain desperately needed a strong leader. Few could deny that in Winston Churchill, Britain had the best it could get. As Churchill himself said, 'The people of London with one voice would say to Hitler, "You do your worst and we will do our best".' However, not everyone appreciated him. We shall see in the following quote from Field Marshal Lord Alanbrook, that it is impossible to please everyone all of the time.

He knows no details, has only got half the picture in his mind, talks absurdities and makes my blood boil to listen to his nonsense . . . And the wonderful thing is that three quarters of the population of the world imagine Winston Churchill is one of the great strategists of history, a second Marlborough, and the other quarter have no conception what a public menace he is.

Notes

1 See Konrad Heiden's masterpiece of reportage written from inside Germany during the 1930s, commonly published under the title *The Fuehrer* (Robinson, 1999); the first complete version of this book was published in both London and New York in 1944 entitled *Der Fuehrer*.

2 There are some who believe that Hitler escaped by U-boat to Argentina, mainly because his body had been so badly burnt.

Chapter Three

Into the Hands of the Russians

'The Russians are in for the bloodiest defeat imaginable before they reach Berlin.'
> Adolf Hitler, to his military commanders at a conference inside the Berlin bunker , 17 April 1945.

By 7 May 1945, there was still a great deal of turbulence in Europe, particularly in Germany. Even as the military surrender documents were being signed at Reims, Soviet troops were pouring across Germany. They virtually controlled Berlin and were behaving with utterly ruthless contempt towards the Germans.

The Russian population had suffered greatly under the German invasion with whole towns being virtually destroyed. Russian prisoners were also treated differently from their western counterparts. Now, the new invaders seemed hell bent on nothing short of revenge. It did not seem to matter whether the German they were chasing and sometimes torturing was in military uniform or not. This was not uncommon across all the occupied territories.

Eliane Plumer was living in Belgium during the war. Her testimony offers some insight into the hardships faced by the populations of the occupied countries:

I lived in a town called Ghent. The whole experience of living in an occupied country meant that my youth had been taken away. My father's best friend was shot, execution style. He was in the Y Brigade – that was the Belgium resistance. My uncle was imprisoned for six months because he dared listen

33

to the BBC. My aunt had already married into a Jewish family. They were all rounded up and taken to a concentration camp. We never saw them again.

I was at college when the war started and I had to get a job because if I didn't have a work permit, I would be dispatched to a concentration camp. Any job was preferable to that.

Propaganda was big business. I remember one time, the troops walking into the cinema, shutting all the exits and forcing everyone to stand and salute while one of the propaganda films was being played. I don't know what they would have done if anyone had refused but I'm sure they would have done something.

We hid a couple of RAF pilots during the war but we had to be extremely careful. We had to watch what we said and what we did. Our neighbours were really nice before the war, but once the invasion happened, they firmly supported the Nazis. And I had a teacher who was very pro-Allies and another who was pro-Nazi. The latter reported the former to the authorities and the Allied supporter found herself in prison. That was terrible. I heard that some of the prisoners even wrote messages on the walls of their cells, using the only liquid that was available – their own blood.

We had no new clothes during the occupation. We had to make do, making clothes out of blankets. That's all there was. Then we would take them to be dyed. Food was also very difficult to get, things like one egg a week, a little bit of butter. But, strangely enough, after the war, food was easier to get in Belgium than in England. I had moved to England after the war and my mother, still at home, used to send parcels of food to me.

I was nearly killed – three times – during the war. One was when I was standing waiting at the station and the planes flew over, firing their machine guns. The postman standing next to me fell – it was that close. The next time it was the British. They were bombing the whole area and I was in the hairdressers when a bomb exploded. Then the third time was at the end of the war. The Germans were hiding under trams and shooting whoever moved in the streets. It was their last ditch effort, to kill as many people as they possibly could. A twenty-minute journey took two hours, trying to avoid all the snipers. But at least I made it home safe.

As the Allied forces moved across Europe from Northern France to Germany, they passed through Belgium. But we did not know whether to welcome them as liberators because everyone was so frightened. As the Allies moved in, the retreating Germans took a lot of people away and threatened to take more if the Allies continued. We had heard about the concentration camps and about the experiments that were being conducted on people, especially the girls. I can't describe what they were doing to girls. It was just <u>so</u> horrible.

Ghent was actually liberated by the Polish and the Canadians. At one time, we wondered whether it would happen because it seemed to be taking so long. My father hung a flag out and a German shot it down. The town was liberated but the war was not over.

Around the time of VE Day, we started taking revenge on those who had collaborated. Some of the women had gone out with German soldiers and we would cut off their hair when the end came. On VE Day, we were so relieved because everyone had been so persecuted. The sight of the German troops with their big boots was enough to terrify you because of the threat they carried and the power they could have over you. But VE Day brought all that to an end. We jumped up on tanks and anything else and everyone was just so happy and thrilled that it was all over. The day was a holiday and we had a procession. We still had processions for many years after.

Between 6 and 8 May, there was a great deal of disparity between the Soviet army divisions. The front-line Soviet troops were disciplined, sweeping aside all opposition but only killing when it became necessary to gain ground for the relentless march towards Berlin. The troops remaining behind, those of the occupying divisions, were far less disciplined. They cared not what they did, nor who they did it to. They were behaving in the same fashion as they had become convinced the German troops had behaved

35

towards their people. How definite their memories were did not seem to be an issue. But there is an old saying about revenge – two wrongs don't make a right.

One girl was raped by seven soldiers in one night, another sixty times in just those couple of days, the first time with her father being forced to watch. The father of one girl, who had been raped twelve times by a passing squad, handed his daughter a rope and she promptly hanged herself.

One German school teacher was known to have advised her class that if a Russian soldier violated any of them, there was only one option. Suicide was preferable to a life of such appalling shame and loss of honour. Rather than even run the risk of falling victim to such a crime, half the girls from the class drowned themselves, whilst others selected either poison, a bullet, a knife, or a rope over a tree branch.

There was one violent scene at Tangemunde, on the banks of the River Elbe. For several hours on 7 May, the German soldiers and civilians had been scrambling along the bridge, desperate to escape from the Russians. They were carrying whatever they could carry but in some cases had nothing. They were frantically trying to get to the other side where they could deliver themselves into the hands of the Western Allies. Then suddenly, Soviet tanks burst through the trees and into the clearing. They began firing on the unarmed German refugees. Some people were trying to cross the bridge as the Russians fired mortar bombs into the crowds. There was fighting and screaming and absolute panic as shells exploded at peoples' feet. More bombs fell on the bridge itself. People were jumping for the relative safety of the river; safe until the Russians started firing into the water.

Even as late as the day before VE Day, the day the surrender document was actually signed, hundreds were still dying. Defeat for Germany was inevitable and the British, American and Canadians, among others, were seen as far more acceptable conquerors than the Russians. It was for that reason that what remained of the German High Command tried, even at that late stage, to offer surrender to the western Allies and not to Russia.

Chapter Four

Unconditional Surrender Policy

'Like spring, victory in Europe came at last – in its own sweet time.'
Time Magazine, Volume XLV, Number 20, 14 May 1945.

For several months before VE Day, many in the German High Command were completely convinced there could only be one conclusion to the war. The Allies, in most cases, simply outnumbered, outgunned and outfought the hard pressed, overstretched and battle weary German troops. The German commanders made many attempts to negotiate surrender with the Allies, primarily with the Allied Expeditionary Force from the West. But, as was pointed out to them, there was to be no room for negotiation. Either the German High Command accepted surrender without negotiation or continued to see their country ravaged by the warfare they had created half a decade earlier. In fact, the devastation being inflicted upon Germany at the end was far more severe than the devastation Germany had inflicted upon its victims at the beginning. Whether that treatment was deserved or not is not really intended for debate here. What is worth remembering is that in most conflicts it is rarely the high-ranking officials who suffer the most.

An unconditional surrender is quite simply surrender without the opportunity to negotiate, without the chance to lay down terms on the table. It is not so much an armistice as a complete backing down of one side against the other.

Germany had little choice at the end. It literally had nothing left to fight with and very little desire to fight on against a foe, or collection of foes, that had so successfully brought about its down-fall. It no longer had any effective armies. The Luftwaffe had been rendered virtually extinct. Most of the Navy was either damaged, sunk or confined to port. Everything had been devastated. It no longer had a political figurehead once Hitler had committed suicide.

Those who took his place tried to hold things together. But it is difficult to fight a war when your population is fatigued and starving, and equally difficult to maintain a military dictatorship when you have no military.

Throughout the end of the war, the German High Command made many attempts to create conditions. The primary condition involved transferring most of what divisions remained to the Eastern front to face the Russians. The intention was to slow the Communists' approach towards Germany for as long as possible while the Western Allies were allowed an almost free hand at entry. This would have sparked much interest with most people. Surely given the chance for an easy victory, many generals would have taken it. But it was not acceptable. It amounted to a conditional surrender. Only an unconditional surrender to all its enemies simultaneously was acceptable.

Chapter Five

End of April 1945
– The Retreat Gathers Pace

'I cannot permit the surrender of Berlin.'
Adolf Hitler, on being asked what could be
accomplished when the ammunition ran out, 29 April 1945.

The retreat of German forces had been an ongoing feature of the war for several months. By the end of April 1945 and certainly the beginning of May 1945, many prison camps had been liberated, including the concentration camps of Belsen and Dachau and the prisoner of war camps at Fallingbostel and Colditz.

At Belsen, the British liberators found horrific scenes of barbarity beyond imagination. Approximately 35,000 corpses were awaiting disposal and about 30,000 living inmates were close to death from starvation. Of those, 300 died each day for the following week, despite the supplies of food and medical equipment. With some individuals, it was the supplies of food that was killing them. It was more than their weakened and starved bodies could cope with. Sometimes even the joy of liberation brought about their deaths. Kindness killed. So many were simply beyond help. One woman was begging for milk for her baby. On examination, the soldier guarding the store established that the baby had been dead for several days, but the woman still wanted milk. The soldier wiped some over the child's lips and the woman, overjoyed, thanked him. She staggered away and collapsed. She died just a few metres from him.

At Dachau, the American liberators were so appalled by the

diabolical scenes they witnessed of piles of rotting corpses and virtually starved survivors, that they took swift retribution on the garrison troops. The officer who first handed over the camp, Lieutenant Heinrich Skodzensky, was the first to be executed. Other guards were killed by some of the more able inmates but over 300 were executed by the American troops. The process took one hour. There was no telling how swiftly those same guards had been able to execute inmates but it was unlikely that the Americans had broken any records.

The Russians had been shelling Berlin since the middle of April. Buildings of every type were damaged, with many uninhabitable. Supplies of food were running out and no more were filtering through. It was estimated by the German High Command itself that Berlin would starve after 10 May.

Hitler had made so many changes to his High Command that it became difficult to know who was in charge of what. Goering was dismissed as head of the air force and replaced by a pilot named Robert Ritter von Greim. General Karl Weidling was transferred from being a panzer tank corps commander to become commandant of the Berlin defences. General Siegfried Henrici, who had replaced Himmler as commander of a prominent army group, was dismissed for failing to scorch the German country in the face of the Russians. Goering and Himmler were expelled from the Nazi Party and Goebbels would succeed Hitler as Chancellor. Grand Admiral Dönitz was proclaimed President of the new Government. It was destined to be probably one of the shortest presidential reigns in world history.

Hitler was sitting in his bunker, resolute to the end, determined never to be taken alive from Berlin. He was waiting for the massive swathe of German reinforcements to arrive and drive the enemy out. He was basing his information on a few pockets of resistance that actually amounted to very little. He was playing with imaginary armies.

He spent his final complete day before his death writing a testimony. In it he detailed his thoughts about the war and placed the entire blame for it on the scourge of everyone – the Jews, referring to them as 'the poisoner of all nations'. He claimed that millions of European Aryans had starved and died in horrific conditions while the Jews had been treated in a much more humane fashion. It is more than likely that he was referring to the gas chambers.

The area of the Ruhr had been taken, as had Vienna, Arnhem, Nuremburg, Leipzig, Stuttgart and countless other places of strategic importance. The Italian Committee for National Liberation had risen up and attacked the Germans in various areas of Italy, liberating Milan. The American and Russian armies had linked up in several key locations, much to the delight of the populations at home.

Some concentration camps were being hurriedly evacuated and the prisoners forced to march at starvation level, like those from Buchenwald. From this camp, 1,000 Jews were executed at Marienbad in Czechoslovakia. It takes less effort to guard dead bodies.

Displaced hordes tried desperately to find loved ones while still escaping the clutches of their oppressors. One such person was Ingrid Pitt, a lady who would later find fame as an actress in Hammer Horror movies, but as a child she faced a very real horror of her own. She explained that VE Day meant nothing to her for she was struggling for her own survival.

I missed the end of the war.

It was three weeks or so before the news filtered through the forest that the Allies had crushed the Germans and it was safe to go home. Home! What did that mean to an eight year old with only memories of overcrowded camps, rank fear of anything out of the ordinary and living in a forest, frequently ill, usually freezing cold and constantly starving? There had been a lot of talk about going home for the last month or so. The sound of distant battles had stopped. Opinion on the cause of the cessation was divided. Some said that it was because the Germans had been defeated; others that they had won. It didn't mean a thing to me at the time.

Another interesting factor to be stirred into the argument was the sudden absence of refugees – farmers and residents of the surrounding countryside fleeing their homes before the advance of the Russian Army or deserting soldiers on the run.

41

They were either allowed to stay, threatened with violence if they didn't move on or, if times were particularly bad, led off into the woods, never to be seen again.

We, my mother and I, had been lucky. When the threat of the advancing Russians compelled the Germans to pull out we had been marched off with the other inmates of the camp. Constant strafing by Allied planes had soon convinced the Nazi guards that being in close proximity to a column of prisoners, which from the air probably looked like troops movements, was not good for their health. After one strafing my mother managed to haul me off into the woods without being noticed by the few remaining guards. It was winter and all we had on were the rags we had managed to scavenge before leaving the camp. On top of that, I had a streaming cold, which reduced my face to a mask of thick mucus. I think I whined a lot. My mother encouraged me with, 'Not much farther,' but I soon began to disbelieve her.

We trudged on through the wood. My mother was displaying confidence she could not possibly have felt. At last even she began to fail. We huddled down in a thicket. By this time I felt too ill to even cry.

Then the miracle happened. Two indistinct figures passed close by. My mother called to them. She didn't care who they were. If we stayed where we were we were doomed anyway. They were two 'partisans', locals who had found it safer to live in the woods rather than be sitting ducks for marauding soldiers from whichever army might be in ascendance at the time. They weren't keen to take us but my mother suggested they either shot us or took us with them. Luckily, they decided on the latter course.

So we joined the ill-assorted group living in the forest in ramshackle huts and waited out the war. The news of its end came with the Russian soldiers. They fed us and took us out of the forest.

It was the start of two years wandering around Europe looking for my father. At last we found him. That was the real end of the war for us.

Mussolini, the Fascist ruler of Italy, had been killed by Italian Partisans. He had met his end in the village of Dongo. With this event, Fascist power in Italy came to an abrupt end. As if to emphasize the point his body and that of his mistress, Clara Petacci, were transported from Dongo to Milan. There, both bodies were hung upside down. On that same afternoon – 29 April – the representatives of General von Vietinghoff, arrived at Caserta to sign the unconditional surrender of all German troops in Italy.

From his office in England, Churchill became increasingly concerned about the situation in Eastern Europe, especially Poland and Czechoslovakia. He felt that the Yalta agreement was being, at best, misunderstood by the Russian leader, Stalin. As far as he was concerned, he had agreed that post war Poland in particular would have a democratically elected government that would contain elected representatives from all the non-Nazi organizations. But the Russians were already working against that, installing a puppet government that could serve them. Millions of Poles were angered by the events at the end of the war and wondered what they had fought for – they had gone from one occupier to another with barely a gap in between.

Chapter Six

1–4 May 1945
– The Noose Closes

'Germany was an industrial giant next to Russia. They'd declared war on England and America too. What kind of people can do that?'

Last Citadel, David L. Robbins

On 1 May 1945, the Second World War in Europe entered its final week. The Russians dominated Berlin, even to the point of having their flag flying over the Reichstag. This event, completed the previous day, was totally symbolic. It implied virtual ownership and was reminiscent of the period when the Nazi Swastika hung from almost every building in the former occupied territories.

There was a great deal of work still to be completed behind the front lines. Clearing up the legacy of Nazi rule was a mammoth task. It involved thousands of military and civilian personnel alike; people like Iris Smith.

Iris started the war as an evacuee, then a factory worker and finished the war years in the ATS, working in the headquarters of Field Marshal Montgomery.

I was working in the nursing department of Montgomery's headquarters. Although we didn't really know why, we were always on the move. We were moving progressively closer to the south coast of England. The reasons and our future locations were being kept very secret, for obvious reasons – D-Day was approaching.

Although D-Day was one day, the landings continued for several days afterwards. Unfortunately, some of those days suffered from bad weather in the English Channel so some crossings were delayed longer than had been planned. When I crossed in a troop ship, it was several days after D-Day itself. The Allied troops were already making head roads into Europe. I landed on Gold Beach with the 21 Army Group HQ.

My first point of call was a field in Bayeaux, where my nursing skills continued. Some of the wounds were really terrible but it was one of those circumstances where you just got on with it. There wasn't really any choice. Conditions there were pretty basic, like taking a bath in an old oil drum that had been cleaned and cut in half; or taking group showers, standing in rows, bodies naked except for tin helmets to keep the hair dry.

As we progressed through Holland and Belgium, following the main thrust of the war machine, we kept having to move our mobile camps, trailing along behind. If we had stayed put, the growing distance between the advancing troops and ourselves might have killed some of the casualties by the time they had been brought back. We received a truly wonderful reception when we arrived in Brussels. Those people had been living under occupation for many years and suddenly they were free. Jubilation was only natural.

I remember one particular building on Avenue Louise. There was a car park beneath the building where ambulances would deliver women and girls who had been made pregnant by German soldiers. They would then be taken up into the building where they would endure a forced abortion. We actually found rows upon rows of embryos, pickled in jars.

On our arrival into Germany, we were able to establish two headquarters, Bad Oeynhausen – the forward HQ, and Herford – the rear HQ. However, from each of these, we were not allowed outside without an armed escort because the locals were hostile. I remember there were wounded service personnel everywhere and one in particular sticks in my mind and will remain with me forever. All he could say was 'If only I could see'.

In the medical facilities, we saw first hand the horrors the Nazi regime had created for its own population and how a once proud and mighty nation could collapse so swiftly into poverty and depravity when crushed from all sides. We had two German women working for us in the medical unit and they were clearly struggling to come to terms with what was happening. They caught us feeding a stray cat some scraps and some milk. When they had the opportunity, they pushed the cat away and ate the scraps themselves and drunk the milk, after the cat had been feeding. I don't think I have ever seen such desperation for food.

I managed to get home just in time for VE Day. I was on a seven-day leave period but found myself having to fly back to Europe for night duty. So that was how I spent my VE Day. Having thought I was going to be in England, instead having to return to the full horrors left behind after peace was celebrated. I was assured I would get 48 hours extra at some point in the future but no one could give me any idea of when. There was just so much devastation and suffering. I should think that, on VE Day and immediately after, I was kept extremely busy and those around me were some of the busiest people. I was working in a hostile land, unable to venture out without escort, tending the suffering, the wounded. It was utterly dreadful but it was a job and it had to be done.

As a consequence of my work, VE Day itself did not really hold any significance for me. I had to go back to where I had just come from to witness more of the same. There was a huge relief that the conflict was over – I won't deny that. But it was not a conclusion. The civilian population in Germany were hostile and of course there was still fighting and suffering and dying going on further afield. Japan was still fighting.

VE Day was a few days away, but there was still plenty of bloodshed and confusion, much of it being at the hands of the Russians. They were still massacring German troops and civilians even as the final surrender was being signed.

46

The German garrison stationed on the Greek island of Rhodes surrendered.

In Berlin, there was very little left of the German High Command. Goebbels was dead. General Krebs, who had earlier that day failed to negotiate a truce with the Russian officer, General Zhukov, killed himself. Professor Max de Crinis, one of those who had established the Nazi euthanasia programme, also committed suicide.

The surrender of German forces in Italy, already signed, became fully effective on 2 May. Among those stationed in Italy at the time was an Allied soldier named Ron Seabrook. He had moved from place to place including Algeria, Egypt and Italy. He had originally joined the Middlesex Regiment as a machine gunner but transferred to the catering corps attached to different units.

I think I was probably quite lucky during the war. I didn't actually loose any family members, although one brother was blinded. But the people I was serving with were very high risk. For a while I was with the reconnaissance corps, up at the front line, finding out information about enemy movements. Every time we moved, we lost people. It was a dangerous unit to be serving in.

When VE Day happened, we were bypassing Cassino and moving through the outskirts of Rome. Rome hadn't fallen. We just bypassed it. I had no idea what my family was doing. I had absolutely no contact at all. Although I was serving in the European campaign, VE Day really meant very little because we were still fighting. Although there had been the surrender, there were still problems. I can't remember having much of a celebration on that particular day, not like there would have been at home. We allowed ourselves more of a celebration of VJ Day. That was better for us. We were in Greece then. That was a great time because it really meant the end of the war.

Grand Admiral Dönitz, the head of what remained of the German *Wehrmacht*, had already started diverting as much military power as possible to try to slow the Russian advance through Berlin. With no possible outcome other than conquest, he advised the German people to welcome the arrival of the western Allies in favour of those from the east. The following day, both Berlin and Hamburg surrendered unconditionally.

Chapter Seven

4 May 1945
– The Surrender in North Europe

'The two young men were sitting on the lawn with a chess table
between them when the radio through the refectory hall window,
speaking in the impossibly posh accent of the BBC newsreaders
in those days, announced that Field Marshal von Rundstedt had
just signed on Lüneburg Heath the instruments of unconditional
surrender.'

Avenger, Frederick Forsyth.

The date was 3 May 1945 and the time was 11.30 a.m. Two senior
German officers, Admiral Hans Georg von Friedeburg and
General Hans Kinzel, arrived at Lüneburg Heath, near the village
of Wendisch Evern. Friedeburg had taken on the role of the
German Chief of Naval Staff when the previous incumbent, Grand
Admiral Dönitz, had been elevated to replace Hitler after the
suicide. Kinzel was the Chief of Staff of the German North-West
Army Command.

Both officers had reported to the headquarters of the British 21st
Army Group. The Commander-in-Chief, Field Marshal
Montgomery, demanded to know who they were and what they
wanted. Whether he was being deliberately patronizing or merely
ignorant is a subject for speculation.

The purpose of their mission had been to attempt to surrender
all the German troops within their immediate authority. This
amounted to about three complete divisions. But they only wanted
to surrender on condition that such an act could be made solely to

49

the British and not to the Russians. Montgomery flatly refused the condition. He informed them that they could only surrender the army groups facing his soldiers. They occupied Holland, Denmark and north-west Germany. Any troops facing the Russians had to surrender to the Russians.

Montgomery then threatened to continue with the war, claiming that he would be delighted to do so. He knew he was onto a winner here. The Germans in those areas had been all but defeated anyway. The German officers had little choice but to comply. They did, however, insist on reporting back to Grand Admiral Dönitz who was at Flensburg, in the north of Germany.

Both military delegates returned, arriving at five thirty in the afternoon of the following day. One hour later, they had signed the instrument of surrender.

The German Command agrees to the surrender of all German armed forces in HOLLAND, in northwest GERMANY including the FRISIAN ISLANDS and HELIGOLAND and all other islands, in SCHLESWIG-HOLSTEIN and in DENMARK, to the C-in-C 21 Army Group. This to include all naval ships in these areas. These forces to lay down their arms and to surrender unconditionally.

All hostilities on land, on sea, or in the air by German forces in the above areas to cease at 0800 hrs. British Double Summer Time on Saturday 5 May 1945.

The German command to carry out at once, and without argument or comment, all further orders that will be issued by the Allied Powers on any subject.

Disobedience of orders, or failure to comply with them, will be regarded as a breach of these surrender terms and will be dealt with by the Allied Powers in accordance with the accepted laws and usages of war.

This instrument of surrender is independent of, without prejudice to, and will be superseded by any general instrument of surrender imposed by or on behalf of the Allied Powers and applicable to Germany and the German armed forces as a whole.

This instrument of surrender is written in English and in German. The English version is the authentic text.

The decision of the Allied Powers will be final if any doubt or dispute arises as to the meaning or interpretation of the surrender terms.

It was the first of the significant surrenders of German forces. This was to become the forerunner to the final surrender a few days later. It marked the culmination of months of struggle across northern Europe and represented freedom for some of the occupied territories. German troops in Holland, Denmark and north-west Germany were to lay down their weapons.

The surrender would take effect at eight in the morning of 5 May 1945. On that day, Holland and Denmark officially became free from the tyranny they had endured for half a decade. No longer would the civilian population face imprisonment or execution for disagreeing with one of Hitler's vicious policies.

Remnants of the German SS remained at liberty in Denmark as late as 7 May. Interestingly, though perhaps not surprisingly, these individuals refused even then to accept the document for what it was. Instead, they claimed that this could not possibly be an unconditional surrender. It was, to them, merely a truce.

There were those with close ties to the conquered and now liberated territories living in the UK, people like Alice Catherina Allison-Krafft. Now known to her friends as Cato, she had trained as an ambulance driver before the war. But as there were no hospitals in Abersoch, North Wales, she joined the Land Army. Her role took her to local farms, where she ploughed fields, milked cows and cut hedges. She was also a teacher.

I am half Dutch, on my father's side. There was very little information emerging from the Netherlands about what was going on there so we didn't really know until afterwards. One of the things that did happen with my family concerned my cousin. To avoid being imprisoned, Pieter van de Polder took the precaution of dressing as a girl.

I was born near Manchester, where my parents owned three bungalows and my father worked as a manager for Unilever. From there, I moved to Wales, where I lived during the war. That was where I met my husband. He flew Blenheim bombers for the RAF and was shot down during one mission over France. *La Resistance*, the French resistance movement, assisted his escape. The assistance he was given by the organization was incredible. He travelled through France from the Somme, past Paris and into Spain, then from Gibraltar to Anglesey and finally back home. I knew he was on his way because we received a telegram – 'Jim fine. Home soon' – Signed Gil.

Unfortunately, there was not a great local celebration for VE Day. It was very low key and there had not been time to make any preparations. Word had got around that the Germans had surrendered but the people in the local area did not celebrate unduly. We danced and drank champagne to toast those who had given their lives for peace and those who had saved us.

I was pregnant, so the significance for me meant that I was able to raise my child in peace. That, of course, was very important. The whole experience was all very emotional for me.

The cessation of hostilities had come in time for many Dutch and Danes but too late for others. The numbers of casualties were, as with everywhere else, horrific. One victim became famous after her untimely death. The aspiring writer Anne Frank and her family were hidden for years in the attic of a house in Amsterdam and were terrified because they were Jewish. They were betrayed shortly before the end of the war and only Anne Frank's father ever saw Holland free from German rule again. The house where they lived has now become a tourist attraction in the city and a poignant reminder of oppression and of a desperate struggle for survival.

Others had been more fortunate. Even as the surrender was taking effect, many Jewish families were being reunited. This was often a difficult process since parents had gone into hiding and concealed their children with trustworthy Christian families. The problem was that this process of reunification and learning to adapt to new lifestyles would take some time. The children had perhaps only ever known their adoptive parents. Their real family was, sometimes to them, an alien family. Often, children became too terrified of leaving the only family they had ever known.

This represented just the tip of the iceberg. It was indicative of what so much more of Europe was yet to endure. It meant that even VE Day itself could not possibly be counted as a total victory. The effects of the Second World War were destined to continue for many years afterwards. Even after all the war crime trials had been concluded, there were still dispossessed people throughout the Continent and many more who harboured ill feeling towards certain groups of people.

Chapter Eight

4–7 May 1945 – On The Ropes

'On the 8th May 1945 the war in Europe ended officially, representatives of the German High Command having signed the act of military surrender. But it must be noted that this surrender was made by the high command and not by the German Government of Admiral Doenitz which, after Hitler's reported death in Berlin, claimed to represent the German nation. Indeed, the Allies refused to recognize such a government and it was later arrested at Flensburg.'

The Memoirs of Field Marshal Montgomery

Germany had annexed Austria in March 1938, considering it merely a part of the overall new nation of Greater Germany. On 4 May 1945 German troops in Innsbruck and Salzburg surrendered. On the same day, Allied troops liberated Flossenbürg concentration camp and invaded Hitler's former mountain retreat at Berchtesgaden.

While being seen to be publicly friendly with Stalin, Churchill continued to have grave concerns about the way Russian forces were moving across east European territories. Poland was already going under, as were Yugoslavia, Czechoslovakia, Romania, Bulgaria and Hungary, as well as much of Germany to the occupational limits. It seemed as though Russia was using its approach to Germany as an excuse to expand its own empire, engulfing the nations sandwiched between. These nations were not being liberated, as those in Western Europe were, but were being re-conquered.

In a bold move, he had already diverted Montgomery to the

prominent area of Lübeck. There, the Field Marshal was to hold back the Russian advance and prevent Russian troops from taking Denmark and the rest of northern Europe. The most disastrous situation would have been for Russia to enjoy total control of Continental Europe.

In southern Germany, on 5 May 1945, another surrender took place. This time, German troops stationed between the Bohemian mountains and the Upper Inn River capitulated. Their commanding officer, General Hermann Foertsch was asked if he agreed that this was an unconditional surrender and not an armistice. He explained that he had nothing left at his disposal to present any kind of argument.

Also on 5 May, German forces occupying south-east Germany and the rest of occupied Austria surrendered. On that day there were liberations of more camps including Ebensee, a satellite of Mauthausen, which was liberated by a staggering force of three American soldiers in a light tank. The liberators of Mauthausen itself, found 10,000 corpses in a communal grave and 110,000 undernourished survivors. As with so many inmates of other camps, many here had already become too weak to survive and died within days of liberation. Again, battle hardened troops from the Allied Expeditionary Force witnessed, to their distress, the horror that had signified Nazi rule.

German troops stationed in Norway had been systematically defecting. For several days, they had been crossing over the border and into Sweden, which had remained neutral throughout the war. On 5 May, a message was dispatched to the German Commandant in Norway, detailing how to contact the Allied Expeditionary Force to declare his surrender. It said:

Transmitter antenna not less than 400 watts
Continuous wave transmission
Frequency – Day 5875 kilocycles. Night 2715 kilocycles
Call signs   Allied Expeditionary Force Authority – JABU
                    Commander German Forces Norway – JEUR
Message in English
Listening watch maintained from 0700 GMT 6 May.

On the evening of 6 May, the German officer commanding troops in the city of Breslau, surrendered. General Nickhoff found that he finally had no alternative but to hand over what remained of his forces, and the city they had once controlled, to the Russians. But the next day, German forces in Czechoslovakia continued to fight the advancing Russian troops. They were making a last desperate stand in and around the town of Olomouc. In Prague, the German forces became powerless to prevent an uprising by the Czech resistance. When both the American and Russian troops arrived, the Americans, under the agreement between the two supreme commanders, were compelled to withdraw. Fighting in the city and its outskirts continued, with the Germans constantly on the defensive against the Russians. After the deaths of almost 20,000 troops on both sides, the battle for Prague came to an end. The Germans eventually surrendered on 8 May.

Elsewhere, on 7 May 1945, German troops continued their bitter and fruitless struggle against the Russians near Vogelsang, in the strategic area between Danzig and Königsberg. It would soon end.

Underwater, the war continued, although on a reduced scale. German U-boats were still active in places, and one accounted for the sinking of two merchant ships in the North Sea. The Allied merchant sailors who died were the last sailors to perish in the European war. By this time 2,800 Allied merchant ships and 148 Allied warships had been sunk by U-boats. A signal was sent by the Allies to all U-boat commanders instructing them how to surrender:

To all 'U' Boats at sea.
    Carry out the following instructions forthwith which have been given by the Allied Representatives.

Surface immediately and remain surfaced.
    Report immediately in P/L your position in latitude and longitude and number of your 'U' Boat to the nearest British, US, Canadian or Soviet coast W/T station on 500 kc/s (600 metres) and to call sign G2210 on one of the following high frequencies : 16845 – 12685 or 5970 kc/s.

Fly a large black or blue flag by day.

Burn navigation lights by night.

Jettison all ammunition, remove breach blocks from guns and render torpedoes safe by removing pistols. All mines are to be rendered safe.

Make all signals in P/L.

Follow strictly the instructions for proceeding to Allied ports from your present area given in immediately following message.

Observe strictly the orders of Allied Representatives to refrain from scuttling or in any way damaging your 'U' Boat.

These instructions will be repeated at two hour intervals until further notice.

Chapter Nine

7 May 1945
– The Surrender at Reims

General Eisenhower, the Supreme Commander of the Allied
Expeditionary Force, played host in name only to the most historic
event of the entire European element of the Second World War.
He did not attend the actual signing of the surrender document.
Instead, he chose to wait in his office for news that the deed had
been done and that Germany had finally surrendered unconditionally to the armed forces under his control. The date was 7 May
1945 and the location was his Headquarters at Reims in France.

He had allocated his war room for the signing. Across the walls
were maps of battle plans, supply routes, communication links and
known German positions. It was vital information for which the
German officers would have done almost anything to have had
access to. In the centre of the room was a table. It was made of
wood, plain and rickety and with the top painted black. It was an
unremarkable table, except for what was about to happen around
it. There were fourteen chairs, twelve on one side, and two on the
other, the latter as if facing an unrelenting panel. The room was
well lit.

The Allies entered the room first, where a selected band of
reporters and photographers waited for the historic moment. All
the officers were making a wonderful attempt at appearing relaxed
but all were clearly anxious. When the Germans entered, General
Jodl appeared very tense. His facial muscles were taut. Admiral

Map of Europe showing some of the key areas that featured in the
Second World War, leading towards VE Day. Some of the places where
the documents of surrender were signed are shown, including Reims,
Berlin and last place of surrender – Slovenski Gradec.

Friedeberg, who had already surrendered Holland, Denmark and north-west Germany, seemed a little more relaxed but was clearly not having a good day. The Allied observers were Lieutenant General Sir F. E. Morgan, Major General François Sevez, Admiral H. M. Burrough, Lieutenant General Walter Bedell Smith, Lieutenant General Ivan Chermiaev, General Ivan Susloparov and General C. A. Spaatz.

Admiral Friedeberg tried the familiar ruse about only surrendering to the western Allies and not to the Russians. This was again refused.

During the proceedings, General Jodl dispatched a message to Admiral Dönitz. It concerned authorizations about the signing of the surrender. It seemed Jodl did not feel confident about being in a position to sign, or perhaps he was stalling. While the reply was awaited the Germans waited in a nearby house that had been allocated to them. The British and Americans took a quick nap to while away the time. The French returned to their quarters. The Russians held a cocktail party.

When it resumed, the Russians were grinning. All the officers sat down at a word from General Smith and the reporters started their frenzied bounding about. It was clear the German generals were growing frustrated with all the activity. General Strong, who was handing out the surrender documents, found the eager reporters were frequently in his way.

At 2.41 on the morning of 7 May 1945, General Jodl signed the surrender and passed it for signature first to General Smith, signing on behalf of the Supreme Commander Allied Expeditionary Force, then to General Susloparov, signing for the Soviet High Command, then to Major General Sevez, representing France but signing as the official witness. This process was repeated four times. By 2.45, all the documents had been appropriately signed. The document read:

> We the undersigned, acting by authority of the German High Command, hereby surrender unconditionally to the Supreme Commander, Allied Expeditionary Force and simultaneously to the Soviet High Command all forces on land, at sea, and in the air who are at this date under German control.

The German High Command will at once issue orders to all German military, naval and air authorities and to all forces under German control to cease active operations at 23.01 hours Central European Time on 8 May 1945, to remain in positions occupied at that time. No ship, vessel or aircraft is to be scuttled, or any damage done to their hull, machinery or equipment.

The German High Command will at once issue to the appropriate commanders, and ensure the carrying out of any further orders issued by the Supreme Commander Allied Expeditionary Force and by the Soviet High Command.

This Act of military surrender is without prejudice to, and will be superseded by any general instrument of surrender imposed by, or on behalf of the United Nations and applicable to Germany and the German armed forces as a whole.

In the event of the German High Command or any of the forces under their control failing to act in accordance with the Act of Surrender, the Supreme Commander Allied Expeditionary Force and the Soviet High Command will take such punitive or other action as they deem appropriate.

It had taken just four minutes for the might of the Third Reich to finally accept its defeat. The reporters and photographers were leaping over each other. One wanted a picture of the Russian interpreter, a tall bald man. The photographer leaned over the Germans, pushing a disgruntled General Jodl out of the way. All Jodl could do was sit there, stiff and unblinking, taking every humiliation. How the mighty had fallen.

Once the excitement had diminished, General Jodl rose and sought permission to speak. He said:

Herr General, with this signature the German people and the German armed forces are, for better or worse, delivered into the victor's hands. In this war, which lasted more than five years, both have achieved and suffered more than perhaps anyone else in the world. In this hour, I can only express the hope that the victor will treat them with generosity.

General Jodl and Admiral Friedeberg were then escorted to the office of General Eisenhower. There, they met with Eisenhower himself and his deputy, Air Chief Marshall Tedder. General Eisenhower asked the Germans if they fully understood the surrender terms. The Germans confirmed that they did. They were marched away.

A message was then released; the most important message of the entire European part of the Second World War; a message millions had fought and struggled for so long to hear:

The Mission of this Allied Force was fulfilled at 02.41, local time, May 7 1945.

It was all over.

Chapter Ten

8 May 1945
– More Activity Yet To Come

VE Day was officially 8 May 1945. Britain and the USA both found themselves in the grip of mass celebration. The cities across Western Europe, cities that had once been held captive by a hostile and murderous force, relived the celebrations they had experienced as each had been liberated. But, due in part to the total confusion and breakdown of communication in many areas of central Europe, there was still a great deal to achieve. Even as victory was being celebrated, there were several divisions of German soldiers still engaged in conflict with either the Allied Expeditionary Force, or more commonly, the Russian Army. In addition, of course, there was still fierce fighting going on in the struggle to bring down the other merciless enemy in the Far East.

8 May 1945 saw German troops in Oslo accepting defeat. Norway was free from tyrannical rule and to this day, thanks the people of Britain by presenting a Christmas tree, which stands in Trafalgar Square in London, each year.

Some Allied troops were already home, including Owen Pannett. He had fought in North Africa as part of the famous 7 Armoured Brigade, the Desert Rats, named after a breed of rat called the Jerboa. He found himself in North Africa in October 1940, fighting alongside the legendary Gurkhas.

I fought under various Generals. There was General Auchinleck, General Gort, General O'Connor and General Wavell, as well as Montgomery. I had arrived by ship, having been assured of three months to acclimatize myself to the desert atmosphere. I had three weeks and then I was in the thick of it.

At the beginning, the Germans were not based in North Africa. We were fighting the Italians and at one point, were outnumbered by eight to one.

Then Rommel arrived with the German *Afrika Korps*. I think that was in 1941. He was far from being a Nazi but was a German soldier doing a job that just happened to be serving the Nazi party at that time. I even recall him apologizing on one occasion to POWs for handing the camp over to the Italians.

We could probably have finished the North Africa war quite swiftly, were it not for the fact that we had very outdated and inferior weaponry. General Wavell kept asking for new equipment and was constantly refused. Churchill wanted to keep the war in North Africa going to distract German attentions away from Europe as much as possible. The same was true for General Auchinleck. So by the time Field Marshal Montgomery arrived, events in Europe were changing and he managed to get more modern equipment, making his task of victory easier.

I was involved in several battles, the most notable being Sidi Rezegh and El Alamein. The latter was the last stand for the British in Egypt. The fighting was intense and we lost so many people – as did the Germans. At one point at Sidi, I even became stranded from my group.

I came home after Italy had capitulated. I had become known by some as one of the D-Day Dodgers. That meant that I had missed the landings. But I had already been fighting since 1940 so surely I had done my bit. I was in England right the way through to the end of the war and on VE Day, I was in Nottinghamshire. I was with part of my regiment and working with recruits, training them. I was actually on the rifle ranges with some of them when the news came through.

Naturally, everyone downed tools – or should I say weapons – and celebrated. We indulged in some quality drinking but there wasn't really much more. You see, although the war was over, at least in Europe, there was still a great deal to do.

I was very aware of the local celebrations. If you travelled anywhere that day, it would have been very difficult not to be aware of them. But, for me personally, even if I weren't still working, I wouldn't have had much cause to celebrate. My closest friend had died in El Alamein. His name was Richard Smith and I shall always remember him with the honour and respect he deserved.

Others in the forces performed their duties without even leaving the UK.

Mary Foreman, formerly Mary Locton, had spent the tail end of the war serving in the Women's Royal Naval Service, which she joined in May 1944, just before D-Day.

I was a volunteer for the Red Cross, one night a week in Chislehurst in Kent. My father worked in Chislehurst, serving in the police force. One of his tasks was controlling and directing traffic from London to Chislehurst. The caves there were used as a huge natural underground air raid shelter and people would arrive literally by the lorry load. At the beginning, each person brought their bedding every night, until finally the process became more organized and families had their own allotted slots. They could then leave items there when they were away during the day. The caves were like a home from home, even containing a cinema. I think there was even at least one baby born in there.

I joined the WRNS service as soon as I could, which I think was one of the best decisions of my life. The comradeship amongst members of the services was tremendous and I still keep in touch with some of the friends I met while serving, even after all these years.

I completed my basic training in the service at Mill Hill in London above a British Restaurant. That was a place, set up by the government, where people could go for a meal that would effectively constitute extra rations. Then I was transferred to Highgate, where I became a pay writer. As I recall, that was around the time the V2 rockets started appearing and we tended to spend more of our time under the desks than behind them. I used to travel to work on the underground and at every station, there were people sleeping on the platforms.

As the war in Europe drew closer to its conclusion, I was transferred to Portsmouth. The beaches there had been scattered with mines and covered in barbed wire. By the time VE Day arrived, some areas had been cleared of such hazards. Those precautions against invasion were of course by then no longer needed. The Germans were too busy defending themselves towards the end to be concerned with further invasions.

I decided to join a crowd who had found a safe area of the beach and lit a bonfire. I tried to encourage a friend to join me. Despite the joyful time, she was very upset. She wanted to know what there was for her to celebrate. The conflict had killed two brothers, who had both been serving in the RAF.

There was definitely the full range of emotions circulating that day. Joy, sadness, relief – you name it and it was there. My husband had lost a brother and sister to a doodlebug that fell on Strood in Kent.

Looking back, I really don't know how we managed to survive and get through the entire dreadful experience. Rationing did not seem to have done us much harm. In fact, rationing probably made people more inventive and resourceful. In the forces, we tended to get a little more food than our civilian counterparts so I was, from time to time, able to bring extra food home, which of course helped tremendously.

On 8 May, another surrender took place. Troops in East Germany handed over power to the Russians. Likewise, German troops in Dresden, a city which had been severely pounded by Allied bombers for some time, surrendered, as did those in Latvia. The troops here had been isolated from any reinforcements and major supplies for some time by the flow of the Russian Army across east Europe.

German troops in western Czechoslovakia were ordered to lay down their weapons. After a three hour wait for a response that failed to materialize, the Russian commander ordered military action to resume. They had had their chance.

Chapter Eleven

8 May 1945
– The Ratification in Berlin

The Russians, who had suffered perhaps more than most under the oppression of the past few years, were not satisfied with the surrender at Reims. As far as they were concerned, it had only been a partial surrender. In fact, they referred to the event as merely 'A preliminary protocol of capitulation'. They wanted more than just one person signing for all three armed services. They wanted it not at the headquarters of the western Allied forces but in Berlin itself. The city represented the last stand of Hitler and of German military power.

So, it became necessary to repeat the process, with a few important changes. There were some textual alterations to the surrender document. It was signed by Field Marshall Keitel, Admiral von Friedeburg and General Stumpff. They were signing for the German High Command. Each represented the Army, Navy and Luftwaffe. They signed in the presence of Air Chief Marshal Tedder for the Supreme Commander Allied Expeditionary Force and Marshall Zhukov on behalf of the Supreme High Command of the Red Army. The process was witnessed by General Lattre-Tassigny, representing the French Army and General Spaatz, representing the United States Strategic Air Force.

This surrender document, signed on 8 May 1945, read as follows:

We the undersigned, acting by authority of the German High Command, hereby surrender unconditionally to the Supreme Commander, Allied Expeditionary Force and simultaneously to the Supreme High Command of the Red Army all forces on land, at sea, and in the air who are at this date under German control.

The German High Command will at once issue orders to all German military, naval and air authorities and to all forces under German control to cease active operations at 23.01 hours Central European Time on 8 May 1945, to remain in positions occupied at that time and to disarm completely, handing over their weapons and equipment to the local Allied commanders or officers designated by representatives of the Allied Supreme Commands. No ship, vessel or aircraft is to be scuttled, or any damage done to their hull, machinery or equipment and also to machines of all kinds, armament, apparatus and all the technical means of prosecution of war in general.

The German High Command will at once issue to the appropriate commanders, and ensure the carrying out of any further orders issued by the Supreme Commander Allied Expeditionary Force and by the Supreme High Command of the Red Army.

This Act of military surrender is without prejudice to, and will be superseded by any general instrument of surrender imposed by, or on behalf of the United Nations and applicable to Germany and the German armed forces as a whole.

In the event of the German High Command or any of the forces under their control failing to act in accordance with the Act of Surrender, the Supreme Commander Allied Expeditionary Force and the Supreme High Command of the Red Army will take such punitive or other action as they deem appropriate.

This act is drawn up in the English, Russian and German languages. The English and Russian are the only authentic texts.

General Eisenhower, who had been in the building the previous day in Reims but not in the same room, was not even, it seems, in the same city this time. He saw no reason to attend the signing of this document. He had already taken the surrender the previous day.

Chapter Twelve

Why Wait Another Day?

There was some confusion as to the exact time to make the formal announcement. Rumours had been circulating for several days even before 7 May but they had all been unconfirmed. Most had felt that, since other surrenders were taking place elsewhere, it was literally only a matter of time.

Hitler was known to be dead. Germany was in complete disarray. The German public were suffering tremendously. In most cases, they had had very little connection with the rise of Nazism, but they were finding life very difficult. No one had warned them that the price of building and losing an empire was starvation, devastation and poverty. Yet, in some areas, they were starving, even to the point of having to find food and water in ditches. Their cities, once mighty and influential in European relations, were being devastated. Poverty was rife as all systems were rapidly breaking down. It was a far more rapid destruction than any economy could take.

The problem was that the Russians, who had provided much of the battle force necessary to deplete the strength of the German war machine, insisted on a delay. The heads of Government of the principal Allies discussed the most appropriate date that would appeal to all. Finally, 8 May was settled upon, although it was agreed that, for the benefit of the Russians, 9 May would also be considered a holiday. They also had to agree the most appropriate time of day to make the announcement so all could make similar speeches at the same time. This was very much determined by the time differences between the nations.

With this in mind, it was decided that 3 p.m. in Britain would be the time the Prime Minister would make his announcement to the waiting nation:

Yesterday morning at 2.41 a.m. at General Eisenhower's Headquarters, General Jodl, the representative of the German High Command and of Grand Admiral Doenitz, the designated head of the German State, signed the act of unconditional surrender of all German land, sea and air forces in Europe to the Allied Expeditionary Force and simultaneously to the Soviet High Command. General Bedell Smith, Chief of Staff of the United States Army and General Francois Sevez signed the document on behalf of the Supreme Commander of the Allied Expeditionary Force, and General Susloparov signed on behalf of the Russian High Command.

Today, this agreement will be ratified and confirmed at Berlin where Air Chief Marshall Tedder, Deputy Supreme Commander of the Allied Expeditionary Force and General de Lattre Tassigny will sign on behalf of General Eisenhower. General Zhukov will sign on behalf of the Soviet High Command. The German representative will be Field Marshall Keitel, Chief of the High Command and the Commanders In Chief of the German Army, Navy and Air Forces. Hostilities will end officially at one minute after midnight tonight, Tuesday.

But in the interest of saving lives, the 'cease fire' began yesterday to be sounded all along the fronts and our dear Channel Islands are also to be freed today.

The Germans are still, in places, resisting the Russian troops, but should they continue to do so after midnight tonight they will, of course, deprive themselves of the protection of the law of wars and will be attacked from all quarters by the Allied troops. It is not surprising that on such long fronts and in the existing disorder of the enemy the Commands of the German High Command should not in every case have been obeyed immediately. This does not in our opinion, with the best military advice at our disposal, constitute any reason for withholding from the nation the facts communicated to us from celebrating today and tomorrow, Wednesday, as Victory in Europe Day.

Today, perhaps, we shall think mostly of ourselves. Tomorrow, we shall pay a particular tribute to the heroic Russian comrades whose prowess in the field has been one of the grand contributions to the general victory. The German war is therefore at an end. After years of intense preparation, Germany hurled herself on Poland at the beginning of September 1939, and in the pursuance of her guarantee to Poland and in common with the French Republic, Great Britain, the British Empire and the Commonwealth of Nations, declared war upon this foul aggression. After gallant France had been struck down, we from this island and from our united empire, maintained the struggle single handed for a whole year until we were joined by the military might of Soviet Russia and, later, by the overwhelming power and resources of the United States of America. Finally, almost the whole world was combined against the evil doers who are now prostrate before us. We may allow ourselves a brief period of rejoicing, but let us not forget for a moment the toils and efforts that lie ahead.

Japan, with all her treachery and greed, remains un-subdued. The injuries she has inflicted upon Great Britain, the United States and other countries, and her detestable cruelties call for justice and retribution. We must now devote all our strength and resources to the completion of our task, both at home and abroad. Advance Britannia! Long live the course of freedom! God save the King!

King George VI also spoke to his subjects on 8 May, saying:

We shall have failed, and the blood of our dearest will have flowed in vain if the victory which they died to win does not lead to a lasting peace, founded on justice and goodwill . . . . This is the task to which honour binds us. In the hour of danger we humbly committed our cause into the hand of God, and He has been our strength and shield. Let us thank Him for His mercies, and in this hour of victory commit ourselves and our new task to the guidance of that same strong hand.

Across the Atlantic, President Harry S. Truman gave the good news to the American people:

This is a solemn but glorious hour. I only wish that Franklin D. Roosevelt had lived to witness this day.

General Eisenhower informs me that the forces of Germany have surrendered to the United Nations. The flags of freedom fly all over Europe. For this victory we join in offering our thanks to the Providence which has guided and sustained us through the dark days of adversity. Our rejoicing is sobered and subdued by the supreme consciousness of the terrible price we have paid to rid the world of Hitler and his evil band.

Let us not forget, my fellow Americans, the sorrow and the heartache which today abide in the homes of so many of our neighbours. Neighbours whose most priceless possession has been rendered as a sacrifice to redeem our liberty. We can repay by ceaseless devotion to the responsibilities which lie ahead of us.

If I could give you a single watchword for the coming months, that word is: work, work and more work. We must work to finish the war. Our victory is but half won. The west is free but the east is still in bondage to the treacherous tyranny of the Japanese.

When the last Japanese division has surrendered un-conditionally, then will our fighting job be done. We must work to bind up the wounds of a suffering world, to build an abiding peace, a peace rooted in justice and in law.

We can build such a peace only by hard, toilsome, painstaking work. By understanding and working with our allies in peace as we have in war. The job ahead is no less important, no less urgent, no less difficult than the task which now happily is done.

I call upon every American to stick to his post until the last battle is won. Until that day, let no man abandon his post or slacken his efforts.

And now I want to read to you my formal proclamation of this occasion.

A Proclamation:
The Allied Armies, through sacrifice and devotion and God's help, have wrung from Germany a final and unconditional surrender. The western world has been freed of the evil forces which for five years and longer have imprisoned the bodies and broken the lives of millions upon millions of freeborn men. They have violated their churches, destroyed their homes, corrupted their children and murdered their loved ones.

Our armies of liberation have restored freedom to these suffering peoples whose spirit and will the oppressors could never enslave. Much remains to be done. The victory won in the West must now be won in the East. The whole world must be cleared of the evil from which half the world has been freed.

United, the peace loving nations have demonstrated in the West that their arms are stronger by far than the might of the dictators or the tyranny of military cliques that once called us soft and weak. The power of our peoples to defend themselves against all enemies will be proved in the Pacific War as it has been proved in Europe.

For the triumph of spirit and of arms which we have won and for its promise to the peoples everywhere who join us in the love of freedom, it is fitting that we as a nation give thanks to Almighty God who has strengthened us and given us the victory.

Now therefore, I, Harry S. Truman, President of the United States of America, do hereby appoint Sunday May 13, 1945, to be a day of prayer. I call upon the people of the United States, whatever their faith, to unite in offering joyful thanks to God for the victory we have won and to pray that He will support us to the end of our present struggle and guide us into the ways of peace.

I also call upon my countrymen to dedicate this day of

prayer to the memory of those who have given their lives to make possible our victory.

In witness whereof I have hereunto set my hand and caused the seal of the United States of America to be affixed.

Following this formal declaration of peace in Europe, the President attended a press conference at which he addressed the problem of the ongoing conflict with Japan:

Nazi Germany has been defeated. The Japanese people have felt the weight of our land, air and naval attacks. So long as their leaders and the armed forces continue the war, the striking power and intensity of our blows will steadily increase and will bring utter destruction to Japan's industrial war production, to its shipping and to everything that supports its military activity. The longer the war lasts, the greater will be the suffering and hardships which the people of Japan will undergo, all in vain. Our blows will not cease until the Japanese military and naval forces lay down their arms in unconditional surrender.

Just what does unconditional surrender of the armed forces mean for the Japanese people? Unconditional surrender means not prolonging the present agony and suffering of the Japanese in the vain hope of victory. Unconditional surrender does not mean the extermination or enslavement of the Japanese people. The meaning is plain. The Japanese had better surrender unconditionally.

I want to emphasize time and time again that we are only half through. The Germans once called us soft and weak. I wonder what they think now.

Chapter Thirteen

The Mood of the Nation

Many people in Britain saw no need to wait for the official announcement that Germany had surrendered. News had already been filtering through and the other surrenders had made the final act more than a possibility.

There were other clues. On 7 May, the Board of Trade had allowed the purchase of cotton bunting without coupons in the colours of red, white and blue. Also on that day, the British Army announced the beginnings of Operation Eclipse. This was the name for the Allied military occupation of Germany. Suddenly, the country that had occupied so many others in Europe was now to be occupied itself.

Although the general population of Britain later discovered that the signing in Reims had already taken place, 7 May 1945 was to become known as VE Eve.

On the night of 7 May, much of Britain was in the grip of a storm. It was very reminiscent of the night before the war started. Then, the rain had been dripping into untested and make-shift shelters. This time, it was unlikely many people cared about the condition of their shelters. They knew what was happening across the Channel. They were ready for a celebration and no weather could dampen the spirits.

Many people awoke to the sound of hammering. It was the sound of jovial people erecting banners and flags. Soon, the Union Jack would be joined by the US and Russian flags. Dustbin lids quickly became a type of musical instrument as people devised ways of making as much noise as they possibly could.

It had stopped raining and the rest of the day would be bathed in clear weather, just right for the party atmosphere that was to follow. There were celebrations right across the country and they varied tremendously in their intensity. Some people went to pubs which were rapidly drunk dry. Others toured streets, being invited into houses for a drink and a chat. Doors remained open for much of the day. Still others hosted street parties. These were hastily organized and made use of whatever limited resources were available at the time.

Thousands more, those with the ability and the desire, chose to converge on Central London. There, the police were massively outnumbered but there were few reported cases of trouble. Most people were heading in similar directions – towards Buckingham Palace, Trafalgar Square, the Houses of Parliament and Piccadilly. There were children perched on lamp posts and soldiers wearing paper hats. A truck would stop at a junction and become swamped in a mass of people who neither knew nor cared where it was heading. A ride pretty much anywhere would be fine. Everything was good natured. Ambulances were standing by but did very little business. Cinemas were shut and barricaded in case joyful crowds decided to go on the rampage. But there were no problems.

There were members of the military from all the nations that had made VE Day possible. Among them were people with coats and umbrellas. Obviously there was more faith in the peace in Europe lasting than the good old British weather. Women were wearing flags in their hats and some were draped in flags. There was singing – one particular song being repeated was *Roll Out The Barrel*. Spontaneously, someone would shout for no apparent reason and the shout would be taken up and passed through the crowd until it became a roaring crescendo.

Some were less jovial. Perhaps they had lost someone or perhaps they themselves had been injured. There was evidence of injuries, with some people staggering along on crutches. Many had little to say to one another, deep in their own thoughts.

Winston Churchill, who had laboured to lead the nation through its darkest period, was expected. On his way to

Buckingham Palace, he stopped to purchase a cigar. It was essential, he claimed. The public had seen him with cigars throughout the war; they would have been disappointed if he didn't have one when he appeared before them on the day of triumph.

When his car arrived at the Palace, the crowd surrounding it was dense. About 20,000 people had converged on the area. The Royal Family – the King, the Queen and the two Princesses, appeared on the balcony. The family could all have left at the start of the war for the relative safety of Canada. There was an escape plan, but they had refused. Their place had been with their people and that was a determination that would give the Monarchy tremendous popularity for years to come.

Almost as soon as they had appeared, to rapturous applause, the call went through the crowd, 'We want Winnie. We want Winnie.' To more applause, he appeared just before six that evening, joining the Royal Family on the balcony, from where he gave another speech, giving all the credit for the victory to the people.

> This is your victory. It is the victory of the cause of freedom in every land. In all our long history we have never seen a greater day than this. Everyone, man or woman, has done their best. Everyone has tried. Neither the long years, nor the dangers, nor the fierce attacks of the enemy, have in any way weakened the deep resolve of the British nation. God bless you all.

The Princesses – Elizabeth and Margaret – slipped out of the palace later in the evening to mingle with the crowd. They remained out there, with their escorts, for much of the evening. People were in London to have a wonderful time. There was a huge party atmosphere with thousands of people rejoicing in the new found state of peace and freedom. A feeling of euphoria radiated through the gathered masses.

The first weather forecast since the start of the war was transmitted that day, as well as a cheerful news broadcast. At nine that evening, the BBC gave an insight into some of the parties across Britain. It was also announced that the Admiralty had issued surrender terms to the German Navy, that British tanks were rolling triumphantly across Denmark, that the Allied Commanders were arriving in Oslo to receive the surrender of German forces in Norway, that the RAF was carrying 350 tons of food to Holland and then flying home the first 4,500 prisoners of war.

Because of the fine weather and British double-summertime, introduced during the war, it did not start to grow dark until around 10.30 that evening. That time, which had for so long been referred to as blackout time, now became light up time. By then, most of the pubs were dry but there were very few instances of drunkenness.

As midnight approached those who were close enough listened for the sound of Big Ben. After the final stroke of twelve, time passed into 9 May and into the era of peace in Europe. It was VE + 1.

Chapter Fourteen

9 May 1945 and Onwards – The Job Is Not Finished

A casual observer could be forgiven for thinking that the job had been completed at this point. But 9 May held its own collection of promises and its own set of problems. Victory in Europe, even while it was being celebrated, still had a long way to go.

There were still some pockets of fighting in Europe, mainly against the Russians. German troops in Czechoslovakia were fighting and did not cease until 12 May. These violations of the surrender already signed and effective were met with stiff reprisals; any German soldier in these areas, if caught, would have been denied his right to be considered a soldier.

Elsewhere there were more surrenders and other places being liberated on 9 May. The Germans on the Aegean Islands of Milos, Kos, Piskopi, Leros and Simi surrendered, as did those occupying the area surrounding Danzig and on the Baltic island of Bornholm. The Germans at Dunkirk also surrendered. The Commanding Officer, Vice Admiral Friedrich Frisius, reported to the headquarters of General Liska of the Czech Army. The German was armed with his own surrender document which he had already signed. Britain's Channel Islands, the only part of British soil to be occupied during the war, were finally liberated.

Celebrations in London and around the country, as around much of the world, continued. Yet, even as these went on, hundreds of former concentration camp inmates were dying. From

Bergen Belsen alone 13,000 former inmates died between liberation and VE Day. Prisoners of war were being collected in temporary bases to prepare for their return home. Yet, amidst all the triumph of transporting these people home, there were disasters. One plane carrying ex-prisoners of war crashed on its way home, killing twenty-five.

Families were still being reunited whilst some people were discovering for the first time that they no longer had any families. The amount of dispossessed people was staggering. The war had created a human catastrophe that was completely unparalleled before or since.

By the time all the concentration camps had been liberated, only 700,000 people had survived. We shall probably never know the exact number who had perished, mainly Jews, Poles and Russians, but we do know that it ran into many millions. From one camp at Jasenovac, out of tens of thousands of inmates, only eighty survived.

East of Pilsen, German troops were still fighting until 11 May, when Soviet troops finally overwhelmed their numbers. In Slovenia, East Prussia and Latvia fighting continued, with several battalions refusing to surrender. Their refusals only lasted as long as their supplies and numbers. Eventually, their enemy overran their positions. On 11 May, the former Commandant of Norway, Josef Terboven, blew himself up. He had joined the long and growing list of German officials opting for suicide rather than face war crimes tribunals.

The troops in East Prussia and Latvia finally surrendered on 14 May, six whole days after their superiors had surrendered all German forces. The last German garrison to surrender laid down its weapons on 15 May. This consisted of 150,000 troops stationed in Yugoslavia. Effectively, this continued fighting delayed the victory celebrations in Yugoslavia until then. They formally surrendered at Slovenski Gradec.

It could be claimed, therefore, that VE Day actually stretched through to 15 May 1945 and that Slovenski Gradec was the most significant surrender, not Reims or Berlin. This becomes an interesting concept. When did the war against Germany end? Was it when the High Command accepted total defeat and signed an unconditional surrender or was it when the last of its troops ceased fighting?

There followed, of course, the massive clean up operation that lingers after any major conflict. There was also the fighting in the Far East. VE Day would have held little meaning for someone locked in a Japanese prisoner of war camp or engaged in combat against the Japanese. But at least 9 May 1945 and the days that followed meant that attention could then be directed against that other merciless foe.

Chapter Fifteen

The Significance of VE Day

'The SS office was told the Allies have interest only in the un-conditional surrender of his forces. Wolff still had to return to Italy and convince General Kesselring, the German Commander in Chief there, of the need for surrender.'

The End of War, David L. Robbins.

VE Day, quite logically, meant different things to different people. It seemed to depend greatly upon what they were doing during the war. Bernard Ledwidge was a child who had spent the war years living with his parents in Huddersfield, Yorkshire. He recalls only three bomb attacks on the town, one hitting a grass bank without exploding, another striking a soap factory and the third landing on wasteland. The bombers were primarily flying overhead on their way to the industrial areas of Manchester and Liverpool. He recalled:

One of my most vivid memories of VE Day was a street party, hastily arranged. The population had been under food rations for so many years and citrus fruits were one of the foods that were difficult to find since they had to be shipped in. It may not sound impressive now, but along with the rest of the food was an orange for each child. There were tables right along Town Avenue and plenty of flowing streamers. It was a real

1. The flags are out at the War Office. VE Day celebrations in Whitehall.

2. Ron Seabrook in Rome on VE Day.

3. J.C. Allison, husband of Alice Catherina Allison-Krafft. He was shot down in his Blenheim bomber over France but escaped capture and returned to England with the help of the French resistance.

4. Troops studying a tourist guidebook to France now the war is over.

5. Burning the midnight oil. No one wanted the VE Day celebrations to stop.

6. There'll always be an England!

7. Here's to the future! Soldiers celebrate their part in the victory.

8. Owen Pannett, standing on far right was part of the 7 Armoured Brigade, the Desert Rats.

9. Owen Pannett at the memorial at El Alamein.

10. Ron Clayton, seated at the front, fourth from the right, at a VE Day street party.

11. Being evacuated was not a happy experience for Ron Clayton. This is the school in Hayton, near Retford in Nottinghamshire, that he attended as an evacuee.

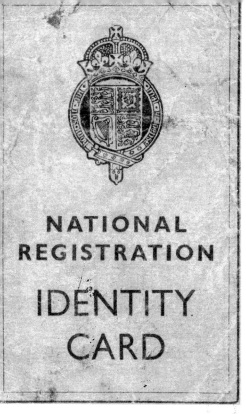

12. The National Registration Identity Card which was issued from October 1939 until May 1943 when it was replaced by the Standard Blue Card for civilians over the age of sixteen and a Buff card for children under sixteen.

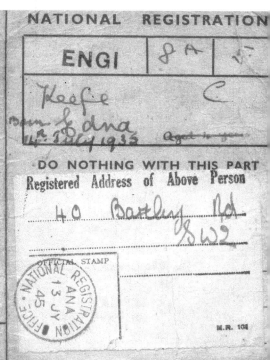

NATIONAL REGISTRATION

ENGI   8A   5

Keefe
Edna

1. This Identity Card must be carefully preserved. You may need it under conditions of national emergency for important purposes. You must not lose it or allow it to be stolen. If, nevertheless, it is stolen or completely lost, you must report the fact in person at any local National Registration Office.

2. You may have to show your Identity Card to persons who are authorised by law to ask you to produce it.

3. You must not allow your Identity Card to pass into the hands of unauthorised persons or strangers. Every grown up person should be responsible for the keeping of his or her Identity Card. The Identity Card of a child should be kept by the parent or guardian or person in charge of the child for the time being.

4. Anyone finding this Card must hand it in at a Police Station or National Registration Office.

51-3120   2

NATIONAL REGISTRATION

ENGI   8A

Keefe   C
Edna
14th July 1935   aged 4 years

DO NOTHING WITH THIS PART
Registered Address of Above Person

40 Bartley Rd
SW2

OFFICIAL STAMP

NATIONAL REGISTRATION OFFICE
13 JY 45

N.R. 101

(Signed)   Edna Keefe

Date   May 23rd 194

14. Schoolboy Brian
    Eccleshall in the
    war.

15. Brian Eccleshall
    now.

16. The party in full swing!

17. Children all over Britain enjoyed the celebrations despite the rationing.

19. Wren Margaret Smith during the war.

20. Margaret Smith now.

21. Margaret Harris became a cipher officer in the WRNS during the war.

22. Margaret Harris now.

23. Actor Angus Lennie who watched people dancing on the air raid shelters of Glasgow on VE Day.

24. VE Day mean't very little to Michoalina Cichowicz. Although her home land, Poland, was freed from German domination, it then had to suffer years of Soviet rule.

25. Marjorie Seelig, front left, with WAAF friends in front of the Great Pyramid at Giza, Egypt in 1945.

26. John Campbell with his ship HMS *Constance*.

25. A symbol of Great Britain's victory - a Supermarine Spitfire.

party atmosphere and a very happy day. There was no more fighting in Europe and looking back now, it was inevitable the Japanese would surrender soon too. All the Allies' attention could be turned against them. I even recall the local grocer using his bacon slicer to slice loaves of bread so we could actually have sliced bread. We felt that surely this was the end of global wars.

I also recall very clearly that sometime during the street party, a Spitfire flew overhead. It was very low, only just skimming above the roofs of the houses. We all ran for cover, terrified that the news had been wrong and the Luftwaffe was using us for target practice. Apparently, although it would be difficult to clarify, the pilot of the Spitfire was the son of someone who lived in the street. That would, I think, have been really nice.

It is interesting to note that the foods that we now take for granted were often not available during the war and Bernard was thrilled to have an orange to eat.

For many, it seems, VE Day meant an end to all the bombing raids. Whilst Germany had ceased its aircraft assaults on Britain some while before VE Day, there was still the constant threat from the V1 and V2 bombs. Had these been developed much earlier, they could have had a far more devastating effect than they actually did. But when VE Day came, there would be no more of any type of bombing over Britain. Virtually everyone in the country alive at the time would have had some memory, or have known someone who would have had a memory of what it must have been like to go to work or school each morning, never knowing whether the house you left would still be there when you returned, or whether it would be bombed at night with you still inside it.

A large number of people did very little to celebrate VE Day. Whether this was through choice or circumstances often depended on their situation during the preceding years. Those in the military were still working, as were those in the medical services, the police and fire brigades. They had very little choice but to continue working. It was 'business as usual'.

Some celebrated with the famous pilgrimage to London; people like William Edmonds, a member of the Home Guard, who manned an anti-aircraft gun.

> I'm credited with shooting down a Junkers 88 bomber, well half the credit anyway. These planes normally had a crew of eight, but only seven bodies were found inside the wreckage. Other Home Guard units combed the area for days to try to locate the survivor, but he was never found. Perhaps the Luftwaffe was growing short of aircrew by then.
>
> At the time of VE Day, I put on my uniform and headed for Trafalgar Square. It wasn't long before I found myself in the Maple Leaf Club. This was a bar primarily for Canadian servicemen. Strangely, they were drinking pints of milk. When I asked why milk, they told me that they could get beer at almost anytime during the war but milk was quite rare and they were making the most of it.
>
> Later, I was growing tired but there was nowhere to sleep. Every area, every shop doorway, was crammed with people, exhausted but not yet ready to go home. I found a concrete air raid shelter. It was little more than a box with a staggered entrance to give maximum protection from bomb blasts. I clambered up and slept on top of this – it was about the only available space I could find.
>
> When I woke, it was still dark. I wandered along Fleet Street and in the distance was St Paul's Cathedral, bathed in floodlights. I think that is one of my most cherished memories – it was so moving and uplifting. For so long we had been forced to spend nights in virtual darkness so the enemy would have difficulty finding their targets. Suddenly, as if the veil had finally been lifted, the area was brilliantly lit. It was wonderful.

Some people had small children and so their opportunity for going out and celebrating was limited. At least for them, VE Day meant that they could raise their children in relative safety. Others, who had been considering marriage but delaying until the war was over, could finally tie the knot, whilst still more knew that they could soon be welcoming loved ones back from overseas.

The division of Germany following VE Day. Apart from a few minor alterations, the British, US and French Zones became West Germany and the Soviet Zone became East Germany.

Even those living in Germany at the time, although undoubtedly saddened that they had not won, seemed to be relieved that it was all over. For them, the bombing raids could stop and they could begin the process of rebuilding. Of course, they were living in a divided country and what became known as the Iron Curtain divided entire families. Those living in East Germany found themselves living under a dictatorial rule that in some ways could rival the one from which they had just emerged.

Eastern European countries were in much the same position. There were former residents of these countries that had managed to escape to Britain during the war and suddenly found that they could not return home. The home they had known no longer existed. It would take half a century to drag itself out from behind the rule of Russian Communism. Many felt let down without realizing that Britain had been almost powerless to halt the Russian advance across nations they had loved so much. VE Day held mixed feeling for them too.

But whatever the impact and the individual memory, let us never forget that millions of people fought, suffered and died to make VE Day a reality.

Chapter Sixteen

A German View

The rise of Hitler and Nazism was completely unstoppable. Few people in Germany had the courage to act against the government, when they discovered what was being done, for fear of arrest and the fate that might follow. A rule by fear became the prime directive in Germany, even before the rapid conquests spread the same doctrine across much of Europe.

The Second World War was, to some German people, 'a bloody nuisance', as pensioner Ruth Sponcz, now living in Britain, would put it.

Ruth Sproncz is half Jewish; during the rule of Hitler and the Nazi party this put her in considerable danger. Her father was a Jew who had been living in Hungary. Her mother was German. At the time when the two married, there was little segregation and no concern about the future. This was before the rise of Hitler and, in fact, Ruth's father died before Hitler came to power.

They didn't know I was half Jewish. Who would have suspected? My father had blond hair and had even claimed on his marriage certificate that he was a Protestant.

My mother and I lived over a chemist. The shop served a certain district within Düsseldorf. In that district, there was a police station. When my uncle arrived, he had to report to the police station. There was a list of known Jews in the area and he was commanded to be included on it. When he gave his name, the police made a connection with me. I did not know this at the time and it was only when the Allies arrived years later and found the list that I discovered that I had been included.

It seems reasonable to presume that had the war not finished when it did (and Germany continued on its path for total domination), we may not be hearing Ruth's words now. The eventual aim of the German High Command was to extinguish all traces of the Jews from Europe and European Russia.

Ruth, like so many others of Jewish extraction, was hoping that they would survive long enough to see the end of the war. 'I was hoping the English would make it quick,' she explained. She had seen the rise of Hitler and the Nazi Party and witnessed the fear and hatred that flowed in close proximity to such a build-up of power.

When the war actually started, Ruth was living and studying in Leipzig. She was attending interpreter school. She had wanted to become a vet. But when Hitler came to power, that choice became impossible. This was not so much because of the problems that Jewish or even half Jewish people encountered when seeking work, it was more due to the fact that, in order to gain access to a university in Germany, each entrant had to prove they were of Aryan extraction. Anyone else, and that did not just include Jews, was forbidden from further studies. This was probably because the rising Nazi party viewed anyone who was non-Aryan as inferior and therefore not worthy of further education beyond a rudimentary level. Ruth could, of course, have claimed to be Aryan, but she would have needed to produce the documents to substantiate such a claim. That would have opened her up to investigation, an investigation that might have revealed her background. In the eyes of the Nazi radicals, people who were half Jewish were just as guilty of causing the disease of the world as those who were pure Jewish. So interpreter school was just about the only option open to her. She could study languages, which would always be useful. Then the war started.

I had very little connection with my uncle, for my own protection. Few people knew I was half Jewish and we needed to keep it that way. My uncle had to wear the Star of David to identify himself as Jewish. Then, one day, he was loaded up and taken away to a concentration camp. We never saw him again. He had been gassed.

Of course, Ruth did not discover about her uncle's death officially. Instead, a friend of his, who had been taken with him, was spared from the gas chamber. He had fought for Germany in the Great War and had been injured. The fighting connection undoubtedly saved his life, because the injury certainly wouldn't have. When he was freed from the camp, he was able to report the death to the family.

Ruth recalls the rise of Adolf Hitler with clarity:

I only wished we could have got rid of him, and I just couldn't stand all that grunting. No, not the Nazi calls for salute, but his grunting. In my opinion, he always grunted a great deal when he was talking. We heard him on the radio and saw him on films. He was always there. His presence seemed to be everywhere. When he visited our town, all the schools had to go out and cheer him and salute. He stood on a balcony and we were compelled to be there.

I think his hatred of the Jews came from the time when he thought he was a talented painter. He wanted to go to a university but he had to pass an entrance exam. It was to see if he had talent and whether tuition was worthwhile. Apparently, the man who tested him was Jewish. He told Hitler that he had shown no talent as a painter.

I think another part of it is that when Germany was blamed for the Great War and had War Guilt placed upon it, the economy was obliterated. The only race of people who seemed to be flourishing was Jews.

We do know that, once Hitler had achieved power, it was made illegal for a Jew to own or manage a business of any kind. Everything was taken away from them – their livelihoods, their homes and, eventually in almost all cases, their very lives. On 10 September 1941, Hitler met with the Hungarian Admiral Horthy and informed him, 'We do not have your Jewish problem'. What he had neglected to mention was that, in that particular area, they had all been either executed or transported. In addition, he even ended the testimony two days before he died with the words 'I enjoin the Government and the people to uphold the race laws to the limit and to resist mercilessly the poisoner of all nations, International Jewry.'

'He didn't like the Russians either,' Ruth adds. 'He was very friendly with them at first, with the Anti-Aggression Pact. But some of the propaganda in Germany was telling us that we should stamp down the Russians before they invade us. He marched into Poland and the Russians didn't like that.'

Russia, of course, was not the only nation that did not like that. Britain was more than upset by the invasion.

In Düsseldorf, where Ruth was living after the war had started, the SS and other authorities were spread out. They would investigate each building and if there was any spare capacity, the occupiers had no choice but to welcome an SS officer, or someone similar. They were not all based in one particular building, in the way troops would be based in barracks. They mingled with the general populace. This would have achieved two goals.

The first meant that they were less vulnerable collectively than if they had all lived in one building. The people would have been less likely to blow up their own house or the house where a friend lived just to kill one officer than they would if all the officers lived together in a dedicated building. The second goal gave the authorities direct access to the lives of the local population. The officer could listen to conversations and search for evidence of treason or uprisings and alert the military in ample time. This method of infiltration has always been a popular substitute when surveillance cameras and microphones are not available.

'There was an SS officer in our house,' Ruth said. 'He was staying in the ground floor flat. The family there had to take him in. When the alarms went off, we all went into the cellar for shelter. Obviously, when he was in the house and not out working, he would join us. We didn't like it. We had a radio down there and we had to keep it hidden. Radios were illegal, especially ones that could tune into English stations. When he was out working, we would listen to the English radio to learn what we could about what was really going on. When he was at home, we couldn't do that and we really resented the intrusion.'

Any intrusion like that would be resented. But it was happening elsewhere, and not just in Germany. All the occupied countries were experiencing similar conditions. However, not being able to listen to a radio was the least of people's worries during this turbulent time.

'He was actually quite a decent fellow,' is Ruth's memory of the SS officer. The organization and the concept of decency seem to be almost a contradiction in terms but, as we move on, we discover why he displayed a pleasant attitude, at least towards Ruth.

> Unfortunately, he took quite a shine to me. When I was going into the cellar, he would always make sure he followed me.
>
> Towards the end of the war, he took me out for some provisions. We rode on his motorbike and sidecar. We found enough to last us a few weeks. About three or four days before the English marched in, he came up to my mother and told her that he was pulling out. But he did warn her that the troops rape everybody so suggested I hide in the wardrobe.

Ruth recalls that she did hear from him again some time later. He had been in Africa and had contracted malaria, which later killed him.

'I don't know how many members of the SS were okay. Probably not many, but there were some.' This, of course, is a very interesting topic and one that has been discussed many times in the past and one which will continue to be discussed, as would the circumstances surrounding the man who had been the figurehead at the start of it all.

What then of the opinion of Hitler, then and now? Ruth explains:

> It was awful. You really didn't know what was going on. Everyone was frightened. People disappeared all the time. Nobody could say anything, except to your closest friends,

because the soldiers would arrive in the night and take you away. And at school, we had to pretend that we thought everything was all right.

Hitler had turned Germany into a powerful country and five years later, it was a mess. When I heard he had committed suicide, I thought that was far too good for him. It was a cop out. He was a coward. I would have liked to do to him what he did to others.

Ruth, of course, would not have been alone in this desire. There were many who had lost a loved one during the war and would have liked to have killed Adolf Hitler in the most painful way possible, or at least seen him brought to trial.

Hitler himself rarely did terrible things to other people. He was not one to get involved personally. He had other people to do that. As long as his followers obeyed his orders and massacred the victims for him, he was happy to declare how wonderful the whole situation was.

'Every morning you had no idea whether you would reach work because of the bombing raids,' Ruth continued. 'And you never knew whether you would have a house to return to in the evening.'

We see many examples elsewhere in the book of people living in Britain, and especially London, being attacked constantly. Bombs were dropping all the time. Yet it is easy for the eventual victor to forget that the other side was being bombed to the same level of intensity, if not more so, and bombs were falling on innocent people too, especially towards the end when what remained of the German military was on the defensive.

'Most of the German people were glad to see the back of the Nazis,' Ruth recalls. 'It was a relief to be living in a free Germany again, to be able to say what you wanted. There must have been a lot of people who supported Hitler at the beginning otherwise he would not have got to power. Once he was there and people started witnessing what the Nazis were doing, attitudes changed. But by then it was too late.'

It certainly was. But what about any attempts to remove him?

'We knew about the assassination attempt on Hitler when it

happened. We heard about one of the people being strung up with piano wire.'

There are two schools of thought on the value of releasing information like this. On the one hand, would a Government embroiled in a lengthy war want the enemy to know that their leader's life had been threatened by his own people? On the other, that Government may wish people to learn about the incident to install an element of indestructibility around the leader. If his own people surrounding him can not even kill him, what chance has the enemy striking from a distance? The German people could be told because this would convince them that their glorious leader, whom they all apparently adored, was powerful enough to survive anything thrown at him.

'It was unfortunate that they all failed to kill him,' Ruth continues. 'Had the attempt succeeded, I think most people, even Germans, would have been very happy.'

From a British point of view, this is interesting because the attempt on Hitler's life, rather than being something to celebrate, would actually have prolonged the war and made victory for the Allies that much more difficult and costly. Hitler knew very little about military planning and tactics, yet he overruled his more experienced generals on many occasions. He allowed his personal ambitions to cloud his judgement to such an extent that his survival actually contributed to the defeat of Germany. Ruth supports this theory.

I think the war could have continued for longer if he had died then. You had generals like Rommel who were completely fed up with what was going on. Some soldiers started as Nazis, but many were cured pretty fast. Others weren't at all. They were ordered to do a job and were actually killing out of self defence.

What you have to understand is that a lot of the ordinary soldiers were frightened too. They were terrified of their officers and of the actual SS and organizations like that. They sometimes had very little choice but to shoot. Sometimes, you had a soldier who, ordered to execute someone, would shoot at them and deliberately miss. But if the officer in charge saw that happening too often, he would shoot the soldier as a deterrent to the others in his command. Obey and shoot or be shot yourself was the way it was.

This also seemed to occur with retaliation shootings. A German would be shot by a local resistance group and in retaliation several local villagers would be herded out and shot in the street. Many of the soldiers, Ruth tells us, did not want to pull the trigger, but had to so as to save themselves. Was this cowardice?

'I was engaged to someone once and he was drafted into the army. He was as soft as anything but he had to kill, or be killed,' Ruth says.

A desperately unfortunate situation. Think about it for a while. Would you be able to shoot a child if the alternative to refusal was being shot yourself? Or worse, your own child would be shot?

At the beginning, when we heard that someone was being sent to a concentration camp, we assumed they were going there for a set period and then they would come back out again. We believed that they were going there to work. There was no information about what was happening inside the camps and, of course, most of the people who went in never came back out again. When the camps were being liberated and thousands of bodies were being discovered, we were absolutely horrified. We couldn't believe it.

When talking about concentration camps and people vanishing because they were not perfect – as a Nazi would define perfection – it seems appropriate to explore this concept with somebody like Ruth. Simply, there was a huge amount of propaganda being drummed into people at the time. Apparently, anyone with a disability wanted to die so as not be become a burden on the state funds.

Oh yes, we were constantly fed information like that. Quite often, disabled people would be sent to special hospitals for treatment. But we never saw them again. People tended to believe what they were being told because the Nazis were so good with propaganda. We were convinced that we were great and of course people wanted to believe that.

Indeed, Germany seemed very prosperous at the beginning of the war. After years of suffering, people genuinely believed that Hitler was achieving great things for the country. Ruth recalls going out to night clubs and having a laugh with her friends. But after a while, things turned sour and Hitler became more and more hated.

I would say that about seventy per cent of Düsseldorf had been destroyed by the end of the war. All the houses I stayed in were bombed. I remember one. The bomb came through the roof and landed on another floor above us. There was a lot of rubble and some went over the pots on the stove. My mother had been cooking but luckily the pots were covered by lids. Food was scarce so my mother didn't want to waste anything. She cleared the dust and rubble off and carried on. We soon sat down to dinner!

There was a great deal of fear throughout Germany about the impending invasion by the Allies. As Ruth explains, she and her friends knew it was coming and hoped desperately the invaders would be marching through from the west.

I was so grateful Düsseldorf became occupied by the British and Americans. There were so many stories of how the Russians were treating everyone. They were uneducated people – well, quite a few of them at least. They were amazed that water was pouring out of the walls in houses. They had never seen a tap. There were so many stories of the Russian troops hurting people as they passed through. I actually knew several women who were in the Russian zone and had been raped by the Russian troops. It didn't make any difference who the victim was and whether they had been involved in the fighting. They were German so they were there for the taking.

The Russian military were on a vengeance trip and nothing was going to stand in their way. They were on a march towards Berlin to destroy the regime that had caused the destruction of so much of their country. Anyone who happened to be in their way became fair game. The advancing troops seemed at liberty to take a little light relief on demand before moving on to the next street, the next town, the next group of victims.

Towards the end of the war, there was very little news in Germany and people didn't have much of an idea of what was happening. This is confirmed in Ruth's account of the V1 and V2 weapons.

'We really didn't know much about them at the time. They were hushed up. People were talking about a wonder weapon but we didn't know what it was. And to be perfectly honest, we really didn't care. We just wanted it all to end.'

This is a strange situation. A propaganda machine, active at the time – some would say overactive – would surely have given out information about how wonderful the V1 and V2 rockets were, and about how they were going to win the war for Germany. This, if nothing else, might have restored some pride. It might have even encouraged a few more war fatigued Germans to continue resisting.

'It may be that some people knew, but I didn't want to know. I was too busy waiting for the end to come. I didn't want to know anything apart from surviving from one day to the next.'

Selective hearing is a useful trait. If you don't want to hear about something, you won't. This also applies to the situation with concentration camps, although there were plans in place to stop news of activities in these facilities filtering back to the general population.

'A lot of the camps were in the east and we certainly didn't know what was going on inside them,' Ruth told us. 'It was only after-wards that we started finding out. When all the bodies were seen and all the other awful things.

'We knew that the Allies had landed in France and later we knew that they were on the other side of the river. In fact, if we could spit far enough, we might have hit them. And when the SS officer announced he was leaving, well that was it. We knew things were about to change then.'

Ruth remembers the arrival of the Allies with some relief.

I recall seeing the troops marching through the streets. We were all talking to ourselves and wondering what would happen now. We weren't frightened but relieved. There might have even been music playing but I can't be sure. There were youngsters hanging around. I hoped they hadn't been told to do something stupid. But we told them to go home and take their uniforms off. 'Get into your civvies,' we told them. Then the next day, the troops came into houses and spoke to us. There was no interrogation. It was a pleasant discussion. They were like long lost friends.

When the Americans arrived, there was law and order. We never had any problems with them. They were not invaders. They were liberators. We were free of Nazi rule. The British followed the Americans and occupied the area. It was then that I met my husband. At the time, he was a captain in the British Army, but had an acting rank of major. He later left the Army and joined the police force, where he finally became a commander at New Scotland Yard. When he was in the Army, he was in the Special Investigation Branch – the SIB – and I worked for him. He was my boss until we got married. Then I was his boss!

While we were being shelled from across the river, there was always a pause. This lasted, usually, about two hours and we learnt from experience that we could then get out and do shopping or whatever before the shelling started again. I think maybe the troops across the river, whether they were British or Americans, wanted a break too.

Ruth recalls the rationing. The Germans found themselves, particularly towards the end, in much the same situation as they had managed to impose on the conquered territories and on territories they were still attacking. The situation was also desperate for the troops; troops that remained alive and free. Few battalions had enough food and ammunition to continue for much longer and news of this rarely filtered home to the public.

'Of course they kept quiet about that. You only heard about it from the troops who came back, particularly from the Russian front.'

Ruth tells us that national pride in Germany, which was low, was gradually restored after the war had finished. People took pride in the rebuilding process and there was a lot of help from the Allies, particularly from America. She goes on to tell us that we have not learnt anything from the war. We still have wars, people still die, and it's all been a terrible waste.

I don't think much about that time now and I think the world should have learnt by now that it's all useless. There's enough for everybody in this world and we could all live together. Then someone comes along and it all starts again. You can't blame a whole nation for the actions of one man. I don't think Hitler was quite right in the head. I think he was afraid of something too. He thought he was the man who could cure the entire world. He wasn't even German but he fought for Germany in the Great War. It's a pity he wasn't killed then.

Chapter Seventeen

The Great Escape

'I am however convinced that there is a God all powerful looking after the destiny of this world.'

Field Marshal Lord Alanbrook, 8 May 1945.

Historians are always frustrated by the cinema, as great stories are embellished beyond recognition in order to tell a story a certain way and feed a particular audience.

When compiling stories for this book, the authors decided to include the reminiscences of veterans of Stalag Luft III, the real-life POW camp, on which the film *The Great Escape* is based. By bringing together a chapter of POW stories, we can capture the different strain of emotions that came with liberation and consequently VE Day.

First, Harold Batchelder, known to his friends as 'Batch', was serving in the Royal Air Force during the Second World War, finishing as a Warrant Officer. He was twenty-five when the war ended and had spent time incarcerated in a German prisoner of war camp. He was shot down while on a mission over Germany. He was, at the time, a sergeant pilot. He recalls:

My Halifax aircraft was shot down in June 1942. I was actually over Germany at the time and managed to remain on the run, eluding patrols for forty hours before I was finally captured. I was taken to Stalag Luft III, the Great Escape camp. While I was there, I was not involved in that actual escape attempt. I had already been transferred from that camp to another by the time of the breakout.

The camp I found myself in next was Stalag Luft VI. That was in Heyekrug in Lithuania, near to the town of Memel. While I was incarcerated, I was involved in forging passes for people planning to escape and also covered for people who had got out. What I used to do was get counted in a hut once, then sneak out to a hut where an escapee had once been and get counted again. That way, the person who had escaped, was given as much time as possible to put a lot of distance between himself and the camp before the guards discovered the act.

I was in Stalag Luft VI until May 1944 when the advancing Russian forces forced the Germans to move us, retreating into Poland. We were at a camp near Ghorun for about two months before we had to move again, this time to Fallingbostel.

We managed to receive news of the D-Day landings. We heard on our highly illegal radio sets that the Allied troops had landed. The Germans confirmed this, announcing that the Allies were promptly and efficiently being thrown back into the sea. Well – that's propaganda for you.

By March 1945, we were roaming around north Germany. The situation was getting serious for the Germans and I think they were considering using us as hostages.

The first proper food we had was in April 1945 when the Red Cross managed to get some food parcels to us. But there was a disaster. While we were sorting ourselves out, we were obviously mistaken for Germans and were attacked by Allied aircraft. A total of thirty-seven of us were killed outright. One of the casualties was a close friend of mine.

But the war in Europe finally ended and we were free. We had been roaming around Gresse and had been seen by a British patrol, which reported our position and arranged for American soldiers to attend to us and load us onto troop transporters. We were each given some chewing gum. Then I had the best meal of my life – white bread, jam and tea. The bread we had been supplied with in the camp was black and absolutely disgusting and when you've been deprived of reasonable amounts of food for so long, something as simple as white bread, jam and tea is truly wonderful.

At much the same time, we were taken to an airfield and then on to Brussels to be de-loused. I was issued with an Army uniform, despite being in the RAF, and some Belgian money, although I'm not sure what they thought we would do with that. Then I was taken to the airport for the long awaited flight home in a Lancaster aircraft, landing at Dunsfold airfield in Surrey. ('Batch' is now the social secretary of the Royal Air Forces ex-POW Association.)

Ivor Harris was born in 1920 and joined the Royal Air Force where he rose to the rank of squadron leader. He spent time in Stalag Luft III. The common notion (according to the film counterpart) is that, in this camp, there were three tunnels being dug simultaneously – Tom, Dick and Harry. There was, in fact, a fourth tunnel, code-named George. Ivor was involved in the digging work for this not so famous alternative to the escape plan.

I was shot down in May 1944, just a month before D-Day. I was flying a Mustang P-51 and was passing over Bologna when I was hit. I was taken to be interrogated and then trans-ferred to Stalag Luft III. There, I got to work on the fourth tunnel. It started at the theatre in the camp and we managed to dispose of quite a lot of the soil from the tunnel under the theatre. You see, like most of the accommodation, the theatre was positioned on stilts to make tunnelling more difficult to conceal. We managed to make great use of the Red Cross boxes during the digging process as the access point of the tunnel had to be supported. Whatever we could lay our hands on and get away with, we would use.

The tunnel was virtually finished and would most likely have been used but for one atrocity committed by the Nazis. The famous execution of the fifty escapees, murdered in a field, became a powerful deterrent and it was decided that no further escape attempts would be made from that camp.

As the war drew to a close, it was decided to use the tunnel

103

as a back up. We thought it was more likely the Russians would liberate us and wondered whether the Germans would shoot us first. The tunnel was therefore to be used as a possible last chance escape route if the situation became too tense. But, perhaps thankfully, the tunnel wasn't needed when the Russians arrived.

I had been moved out to a camp known as Stalag Luft IIIa. That was at Luckenwalde, near Berlin and that was where I remained until the end. I was still in that area on VE Day. The Russians had arrived about three weeks before and occupied the territory. But they did not actually release the prisoners, preferring to hold us as political prisoners, looking for some kind of trade off. So I spent that time not as a prisoner of the Germans or as a freed ex-prisoner, but as a prisoner of the Russians.

Years later, when I visited the site where Stalag Luft III once was, I was encouraged by the welcome I received from the locals. The camp is near Sagan in Poland and there is a museum nearby, where I encountered some school children who seemed very interested. They saw the example we had left, the example of the fight for freedom, as a very important example.

John Banfield (veteran of Bomber Command and Stalag Luft III) feels that,

> . . . young people today are interested in what their parents endured. There are a lot of organizations helping keep the memory alive. In particular, the Imperial War Museum, who are doing a great job in increasing peoples' awareness of the two world wars of the twentieth century. In Poland, children certainly know what happened and are encouraged to look after the graves of the war dead. As a nation, I have found Poland very keen on visits from the British, which is good.

John trained with the RAF in Hampden and Anson aircraft before moving onto Lancasters. 207 Squadron transferred to Lancaster (from Manchester) bombers in 1942. John was twenty-four years

104

old when the war ended, having been shot down and captured by the Germans. Amazingly, he even knows the name of the pilot who scored the hit that brought his aircraft crashing to the ground in Germany.

I started as a wireless operator before training to be a bomb operator. I had a lucky escape – three days after I transferred from one crew to another, the aircraft I had been in was shot down and the entire crew was killed.

I had previously been involved in the famous Thousand Bomber Raid that targeted, among other places, Essen. It was a ninety-minute raid and the targets had been hit so decisively that there was very little defence left by the time I reached the zone.

I was flying in a Lancaster Bomber when I myself was shot down. The attacker was named Manfred Meurer, a pilot ace who was later killed in a collision with another Lancaster. I hit the ground of Germany in January 1943.

When my aircraft was hit, I left through the shell hole and recall seeing the aircraft as little more than a ball of flames. I don't remember opening the parachute but I guess I must have because the next thing I knew, I found myself hanging from a tree, lacking the energy to free myself. When I was lowered down, I was lashed to a ladder and carried to a farm-house. I was then taken to Venlo Airfield, then a rail station where I encountered our navigator. He had hit the tail of the plane on the way out. From there, I was transferred to a Luftwaffe hospital in Amsterdam. I had concussion and a wrenched shoulder and up until then I had not endured any interrogation. But that was not to last. It started as soon as I was transferred to Frankfurt. Interestingly, and perhaps worryingly, the Germans knew all about me before I had even arrived. Maybe careless talk in pubs.

I found myself on a train to Poland. There, I was placed into Lansdorf Camp and Stalag 8B (344), which contained the largest number of British prisoners of war and was about a square mile in size. There were also Canadians there.

When we learnt about D-Day, we initially heard the

English version. The guards, at first, were not concerned about us hearing the news from England because they were utterly convinced that the Allies were being thrown back into the sea and that the invasion was a complete disaster for us. When they discovered this belief was not quite correct, they made every effort to stop us listening to any further news.

Bribery and corruption were rife throughout the camp. When a guard was persuaded to supply something he perhaps should not have, in return for something else, we could then use that indiscretion against him. Blackmail was a useful tool in obtaining a variety of items. The one thing many of the Germans seemed to fear most, and what held many in check, was the prospect of going to the Russian Front. The Russians, they thought, were fanatics who would stop at absolutely nothing. One guard told me that, while the Allies would use a tank to neutralize a machine gun post, the Russians would use 200 soldiers, and not be too concerned if most of them died. It is no wonder they lost so many people during the war when that is an example of their battle tactics.

As the war drew to an end, we were forced out of Poland and into Germany. The Germans were clearly pulling back ahead of the advancing Russian Army. We travelled in cattle trucks, with fifty-six men cramped into each truck. We moved for three days, with no food and stops only for natural essential functions. You know the kind. Then the Russians arrived at the camp where we were staying. They travelled in tanks and lorries. I don't think the tanks even stopped. They simply drove straight through. Some of the Russian soldiers were female and, as it turned out, many of them were illiterate. All the Russian soldiers, male and female, Caucasian and Mongol, were forbidden from fraternizing with us. We were capitalists and therefore not worth conversing with.

Two days before VE Day, the Americans sent lorries to collect us. The Russians fired at them. This was their territory and we were a useful exchange product. The lorries had to retreat, although ambulances were allowed through to retrieve our wounded.

On VE Day itself, I was in the camp. The tune *Land of Hope and Glory* was being played over the loud speaker. And it was played again, and again, and again. Even something like that, after several renditions, became tedious. To while away the time, we decided to hold a soccer match. We challenged some Dutch prisoners and I really can't remember who won. It was just important that we were actually able to play, although we could only manage twenty minutes because we were so malnourished.

Picture the scene – football being played by people barely able to chase a ball, new guards ordered not to communicate with capitalist prisoners, *Land of Hope and Glory* being repeated and repeated and repeated. It would have made quite a spectacle to an observer.

Once I had returned home, via Brussels, I became aware that my family had not celebrated VE Day. They were waiting for news of me and had not heard much. How could they have celebrated under those circumstances?

Matthew Gibb, a flight lieutenant in the Royal Air Force, was twenty-five years old when the Second World War came to an end. He had spent the last couple of those years as a prisoner of war in a German camp. Although he did not escape from Stalag Luft III, he was heavily involved in the preparations.

Yes, I was in Stalag Luft III while the tunnel for the Great Escape was being dug. I had two roles to play. I, along with many others, was responsible for disposing of soil from the digging work. But I was also one of the lookouts. I was stationed in one of the corner huts and from there had an ideal vantage point to look for signs of the guards moving about. Although I was involved in the development of the tunnel from an early stage, I knew then that I was not sched-uled to be one of the prisoners through the tunnel on that now famous night. There were others far higher on the list than I was but I still had my duty to perform.

I had been caught in 1943 and, like so many other prisoners, spent some time being shuffled from one camp to another. As well as Stalag Luft III, I was also held in Tarnstadt camp and then another – I don't remember the name – before being liberated. By then, because it was known that the war was nearly over, our senior officers ordered us not to try any more escape attempts. Although as prisoners of war, it was our duty to try to escape, such further attempts that may result in death were considered foolish under the circumstances.

I was near Hamburg by the end of the war, literally just awaiting liberation. That wonderful time came when I saw three British armoured trucks. It was a wonderful feeling, to finally be free and to know that the whole war would soon be over. Nearby, there was a Mercedes being driven by German officers. Well, we made sure they were turfed out pretty quick. We drove to Lüneburg, where we encountered more British. There was a wing commander who seemed to take a shine to the car so we made a deal. He could have the car in return for seats on the next plane going to the UK. In our eagerness to return home, that seemed like a fair trade.

As VE Day rapidly approached, I was flying back home. There was a short stop in Belgium before I finally landed back in England. I spent the actual VE Day itself – 8 May – in a receiving camp in the UK. I was being kitted out, debriefed and carefully brought back into the fold – so to speak – so I could be returned to my family. I hadn't seen them for the last couple of years and now I could. VE Day was just such a wonderful day because of that.

Thinking about how we were treated, the guards really weren't that bad. They had a job to do and they did it. I had been captured for stealing a bicycle before I entered the first camp and was confined to the cooler – a cell within the camp – for fourteen days. As a whole, we were often up to something and the guards always had to think of new punishments. One morning in the depth of winter, they decided to deprive us of our heaters. As a countermeasure, we stoked one with extra fuel to make it even hotter before they could take it. The guards who came to remove the heater burnt themselves and from then on, the heaters remained in the huts with us.

I think these days there is still a lot of interest about the war and the exploits of some of those involved in it. It was a huge thing and there was so much happening. There is a great quantity of information about various aspects of the war so there must be a lot of interest still, mustn't there.

Richard Yates, born in 1922, was serving in the Royal Air Force during the Second World War. He rose to the rank of warrant officer and spent some of the years of the war in several German prisoner of war camps, including Stalag Luft III.

I was flying in a Halifax aircraft when I was shot down. I was actually on my way home after a mission and was flying over Belgium. I was due to go on leave once I arrived back in the UK before a posting to the Middle East. Of course, I never made it home on that occasion and ended up as a prisoner of war.

I was moved around a lot, being transferred from one camp to another. I spent time in Stalag Luft III near Sagan, Stalag Luft VI, Thorn in Poland and Fallingbostel, which was near Belsen. I was transported to the last one by cattle truck. I think the Germans were trying to get to Lübeck but I'm not sure they knew what to do with us, especially towards the end.

While I was in Stalag Luft III, I was involved in preparations for the Great Escape. I was one of the operators of the air pump down inside the tunnel and was also one of the many who were tasked with disposing of the dirt from the digging. We used bags within our trousers, just like in the film.

During my time there, I reached the age of twenty-one and my coming of age was celebrated during the morning parade. I was called out and presented with the traditional key to the door – a small makeshift key covered in silver foil from cigarette packets. You see, we made do with whatever we could find. A little while after that, before the Great Escape actually happened, I was transferred out of the camp and onto Stalag Luft VI.

I do recall seeing, off in the distance when we were

somewhere near Fallingbostel, the exhaust from V2 rockets as they were being launched. Of course, we had no idea at the time what they were and certainly did not realize they were flying bombs, on their way to England.

I think the Germans, towards the end were going to use us as hostages in some kind of last stand against the Allies. That, of course, didn't really work and while being marched from one camp to another, we were liberated. As we approached Fallingbostel, the British Sixth Airborne Division located our guards and us. That was the end of our incarceration and the start of our freedom.

On VE Day, I was waiting to be flown home. I had travelled to Lüneburg by lorry. In fact, on that journey, we drove and the Germans walked. The tide had certainly turned. We drove across the Elbe via a pontoon bridge. In our collection point, the Americans, we observed, always seemed to have priority on the travel arrangements. They were treated to such food luxuries as hot doughnut rings and it was only after the Americans were on their way that we had our supplies of doughnuts. I recall having about six doughnuts and being violently sick immediately afterwards. We had not been spared much food in the camp and certainly nothing as rich and sweet as doughnuts.

Once I had arrived back in the UK, I was given extra food rations. As I recall, all the ex-POWs were given extra rations. I suppose they wanted to build our strength up as fast as possible. I remember being sprayed with DDT powder in an effort to kill any lice that had decided to travel with us. I'm not sure how successful that was.

Looking back, I don't really think much thought is given to prisoners of war and their hardships. Much is made of the problems back home, and yes, they were severe, but POWs seem to have been all but forgotten. I would like to mention, though, the important and life saving role of the Red Cross, particularly the Red Cross from Switzerland and Sweden. I doubt whether many of us would have survived our ordeal without the supplies we received from those wonderful and truly selfless organizations.

These stories clearly show the passion of the young in times of hardship, faith in the face of adversity and each are an inspiration when looked at in the context of VE Day – the dark cloud of evil lifting from the face of Europe. As Alanbrook observed 'there is a God'.

The next story concerns the recollections of Angus Lennie, who played Flying Officer Archibald Ives in the film, *The Great Escape*.

Angus Lennie was a child during the war and was one of the many children to be evacuated.

Along with the entire school, I was sent from Glasgow, where I was living, to Kinross. I was nine years old. My father had been in the First World War. During the Second World War, he was working in a munitions factory.

I didn't enjoy the evacuation situation. I was an only child. I was only away from home for about six months and when I came back, strangely enough, that was when the bombing really got going. Being a very industrial based town, Glasgow was attacked on a regular basis.

On the night of VE Day, I went to George Square, one of the main centres of the city. I was there with my father, mother, uncle and aunt. It was a real family time. There were quite a large number of air raid shelters there and on that particular day, people were dancing on top of them. I think one of the main significances for me about the day was that it meant I could move on and pursue my dreams. I was a dancer by then and really wanted to enter the acting world. I could, when circumstances permitted, go to London. I used to go to the cinema during the war and watch whatever film was showing and think that I could do that. The end of the war, coming when it did, coinciding with the age I was at the time, enabled me to move forward. It had helped to give me the strength of character I needed for such a career choice.

It is very difficult for me to understand what was really going on during the war and what the whole conflict was all

111

about. I wasn't interested in politics and what Hitler was trying to achieve. I was more interested in what people like Arthur Askey and Richard Murdoch – two radio comics on a show called *Bandwagon* – were doing to entertain us. That was more real to me.

Chapter Eighteen

The Problem of Poland

'We're off to Poland, to thrash the Jews.'
Slogan on a rail carriage carrying German troops into
Poland, September 1939.

The German invasion of Poland is widely viewed as the start of the Second World War. Suddenly, the world experienced a new version of warfare – Blitzkrieg – lightning war. The concept was to unleash a massively devastating assault. Such overwhelming and superior forces would arrive so swiftly that any defence had little or no time to react. Defending aircraft would be destroyed on the ground. Troops would be killed or captured while still in their barracks. Ships would be sunk or scuttled while alongside their jetties. Civilians would be thrown into such a state of panic that their sheer numbers would clog the roads. They would bring any defending military forces that could respond to a grinding halt.

First, the attacking air power would begin to flex its muscles. Wave after wave of fighters and bombers would rain devastation down upon the primary communication links of a country and the main cities. Storage depots would be obliterated. A random selection of houses would be flattened. This was intended, and succeeded, to cause wide-spread pandemonium. Then further aircraft, mainly dive-bombers, would attack. They would pick off at will groups of fleeing people, cutting defenceless civilians to pieces.

Even as this happened soldiers would be pressing hard with the ground offensive. Many of the refugees would find further escape cut by columns of mechanized units, flowing across the country. These would be backed up by infantry who would fill in the gaps. The infantry would become the primary occupation force.

It was a straightforward, no nonsense strategy that would be repeated to great effect in several other countries. In fact, it only really became unravelled when the attempt was made to invade Russia. But there were other factors hindering the success of that particular campaign.

The date was 1 September 1939. As with Austria before it, Poland would become a victim of the rapid growth of the German Third Reich. Much of it would eventually find itself swallowed up in the new nation of Greater Germany, erased for a time from the European map. But the crisis that would quickly become the Second World War actually started a day earlier.

The first victim of the war was a prisoner from a concentration camp. These facilities had already been established and more were to follow. However, this one man was marched out to the town of Gleiwitz, on the border between Germany and Poland. He was dressed in a Polish military uniform and was shot dead. The ruse was an attempt to gain credence for the invasion that would start the following day. The German High Command would later claim that Polish troops had attacked the radio station in the town and the invasion was some form of defensive move. The Germans even had a body, dressed in a Polish uniform, to prove their case. The exercise was named Operation Himmler, after the man who had devised such a sham.

But there were other problems at the time that have thus far been given very little attention. From the east, Russia was knocking on the Polish door. Germany had become allied with Russia and together the two had established the division of Poland. Unfortunately, Poland knew nothing about it. In fact, the rest of the world apparently knew nothing about it. Or if they did, they were keeping a very low profile.

Our first Polish citizen recalls her life during those turbulent times with vivid clarity. She is able to provide us with a valuable insight into the way the Second World War had started. Irena Palmi was a teenager in 1939. She should have been doing what most other teenagers now take for granted. She should have been enjoying life to the full with friends and family. Instead, like millions of others, she was faced with years of subjugation by a hostile and violent occupying force. She had to grow up fast.

'I was living in East Poland,' she begins. 'The Russians occupied that whole area at first, even before the Germans. At the time, we were completely unaware of the Anti-Aggression Pact that had been agreed between the Russians and the Germans.'

Germany and Russia divided a plot of land they felt they had a right to share. That plot of land happened to be Poland. They agreed on a line through the nation. From the German point of view, Hitler saw the invasion as merely a step in the right direction towards reclaiming what Germany had lost at the end of the Great War. It was also a step closer to his eventual target – Russia itself.

For the moment, his two primary aims were to gain immediate control of Warsaw and Danzig. In the case of the former, it always creates an important psychological blow to defenders when their capital falls. The latter city, being on the Baltic Sea coast, was a strategically vital sea route. But it was also an important morale booster back home in Germany. Many Germans felt that the area of Danzig belonged to Germany.

The Russians were also keen to claim territories they were convinced they had lost during the past few years.

'I was working in a hospital,' Irena continues. 'There were some really terrible things happening there. No one knew what was really going on. But we did become aware of some things, like when it was declared that the hospital no longer existed. What could we do with all the patients? They had to be thrown away. Yes – thrown away. I don't know why they did that and what happened to those unfortunate people. We begged for it not to happen, but what could we do?'

This decision was taken before the Germans even arrived. It appears that the Russians had as little regard for the population as the soon to arrive Germans. As Irena tells us, no one knew what was going on. It is unclear what happened to those patients.

'When Germany invaded and started working its way across towards Russia, we had no idea what to do. I was told to spend as much time as possible in school because that was seen as the best way of defending myself. Being in school would offer me some protection from the invading troops. I was also a member of the Girl Guides.'

Irena's assumption that her attendance at school or her membership of the Girl Guides would protect her has subsequently been proved to be quite wrong. Hitler disliked the scouts and guides. In fact, he harboured serious reservations about any organization that was not directly under his control, such as the Hitler Youth. It was reported that on 4 September 1939, in Bydgoszcz, several boy scouts were lined up against a wall and shot.

'As the Russians pulled out, I was taken along with them. I was sixteen or seventeen and I was transported to Russia where I was put to work in the forests, cutting trees. When I had completed a year or so of that, the Russians set me free. I think that was because everyone watching us was needed to fight against the advancing Germans.'

At this juncture, the German invasion of Poland was complete and the invasion of Russia was in full swing. But they were destined to discover that this next stage was not going to be as straightforward. In such a vast country, Blitzkrieg had become impractical and the golden rule had not been followed – Never invade Russia in the winter. Those troops who could, were eventually forced to pull back to their existing territory of Poland.

'I tried to enter the Polish Army. But that proved quite difficult. Although I was eighteen, everyone seemed to think I was thirteen. I suppose I looked a lot younger than I actually was. And all my personal documents that could have proved my age had been lost long before.'

At the time, you were effectively nobody without your personal documents.

'Russia was very dirty, absolutely filthy. There was a lot of disease circulating. I caught typhus and then an infestation of lice.'

Unfortunately, Irena was not alone with this condition. It is not known exactly how many people contracted diseases during the war years, but the figure would run into several million. The living conditions for people constantly on the move would have been horrendous and bacteria thrive in these conditions. This is especially true of some of the water based bacteria. Public utilities

116

broke down at a rapid pace. The welfare of the local population became increasingly less important to the invaders. We see evidence of this in a communication between officials in the Racial Political Office in Berlin and the Nazi leaders, which said, 'Medical care from our side must be limited to the prevention of the spreading of epidemics to Reich territory.'

Irena continues.

When I finally did manage to join up, I was in a Polish regiment within the British Army, serving mostly in Russia. Then we moved back further, converging on Persia, now called Iran. Then we moved to the Middle East where I left the Army for a while to resume my studies. My schooling had been interrupted before.

I was in Nazareth on VE Day. Although the war had finished for most in Europe, for the Polish people, the suffering had not. So naturally, there was no real reason to celebrate. Certainly, the school I was in did not do any celebrating. Germany had surrendered but Russia now owned Poland. We had managed to go from one occupier to another and the whole thing left me wondering what could happen now.

VE Day enabled me to complete all the studies I wanted and go to university. I wanted to be a teacher. I was a lab technician and really wanted to teach. The end of the war enabled that.

At least we fared much better after the war. Although we were destined to be suppressed by the Russians, at least we weren't so harshly treated as we were by the Germans.

This sense of disappointment at what happened to Poland is a common theme running through many stories from Polish people. They clearly felt betrayed by the conditions of the Yalta Agreement. They exhibit few inhibitions about blaming Churchill for what they view as a failure on his part to protect their interests.

The situation in Poland during the German occupation was horrendous. This was never more so than at the beginning. The conquerors were pressing home their superiority. They were demonstrating that their principal method of control was to rule by fear. There were dozens of examples of utter brutality that would astound most people.

In the town of Swiecie, several Poles were escorted to a cemetery. The group included children. There they were shot. When three of the German soldiers watching protested, their comments were relayed to Berlin. The response was that 'you cannot fight wars with the methods of the Salvation Army'.

In Turek, Jews were taken to a synagogue and made to crawl along the floor, singing while their guards whipped them.

In Wieruszow, twenty Jews assembled under guard in the market. When the daughter of one man tried to get near her father, a German ordered her to open her mouth as a punishment for her impudence. He inserted the barrel of his gun into it and pulled the trigger.

In Piotrkow, invading soldiers torched a row of Jewish homes. As the occupants fled the flames, they were gunned down by the soldiers waiting outside. One house that escaped the fire was broken into and the people inside were herded out into the street. They were given the chance to run and, as they did so, they were shot.

There was an official line on all of these atrocities, and many others besides. The problem of guerrilla warfare was being stamped out wherever it rose. The perpetrators were being hounded down and eliminated. The Germans had dispatched emergency law courts to deal with the criminal element. The commanders assured whoever cared to listen that peace would soon be established in the turmoil of Poland.

On the battlefield too, the rules of war were being disregarded. These rules had been laid down by the Geneva Convention. They demanded that military personnel, once they had surrendered, were to be treated in a certain way. They are most certainly not to be locked in a shed and burnt alive, as was witnessed near Mrocza.

But there is compelling and first hand evidence that the German forces were not the only troops to be glorifying such slaughter. Edward Szczepanik was born in Poland during the Great War. He was in the Polish Army at the start of the Second World War. His recollections of the events before and during the war, and his feelings about the end make very serious reading.

> I joined the army in Poland before the start of the Second World War. Almost straight away, I was posted to Lithuania. You see, Lithuania was still an independent country at that time. It had not been swallowed up by the Soviets. When the Russians entered Lithuania, all the Polish soldiers were interned in camps. Controlled by the Russians, we were all destined for execution. There were 5,000 Polish troops executed by the Russians and I was one of the few to survive.
>
> They were simply cut down. In fact, I was in the next batch scheduled for death when the Germans started moving in. The Russians then tried to blame the executions on the Germans. But the German forces had not even reached the area by then. It was the German troops who discovered the mass graves.

The German invasion of Poland actually saved Edward's life. This flows contrary to so many other accounts where the Germans appeared to be killing more than they were saving, at least on the surface. Edward went on to say:

> The Germans continued with their invasion of Russia. They had already taken Poland. The Russians tried to reach an agreement with our General. He wanted what remained of our numbers to fight against the Germans. So we were being asked to fight for the protection of people who had killed many of us.

Before the Second World War, Russian forces devoted a great deal of time to murdering their own people. They would then try to cover the fact. They would demand that Russian murder Russian and then expect the troops to fight alongside those who had just killed their families. So it seems logical to assume that they were also willing to expect Polish soldiers to emerge from watching their friends die and fight alongside the people who had murdered them.

Edward goes on to explain what actually happened with those of his comrades who remained alive.

119

What actually happened in the end was that we were released and went to fight alongside British forces. We were dispersed all over, mainly across the Middle East. Towards the end of the war, as we were driving the Germans back, I was posted to Italy. By then, I had been promoted to captain in the Artillery Regiment. I remained in Italy right up to the end of the war.

When VE Day arrived, it came with a price for the Polish people. The Yalta Agreement left very little opportunity for us. By the time I learnt the implications of this, I had already been sent to Britain to be demobbed. I settled in Britain. I became a teacher. There didn't really seem to be much of a choice. I had no desire to return to Poland under the new regime. Although I would have liked to return, I had no wish to be controlled by Russia. That was the situation I felt I would encounter and find myself living in. A lot of Poles had fought alongside the British forces during the war and the country had been let down considerably afterwards. Churchill was a great leader for Britain but Poland did not fare so well.

The Yalta Agreement was reached between Churchill, Stalin and Roosevelt. They had conferred in the Crimea about what would happen to each area of Europe after the defeat of Germany. Churchill actually had serious concerns about the way the Russians were interpreting the agreement. He told Stalin, 'I have been much distressed at the misunderstanding that has grown up between us on the Crimean Agreement about Poland.'

Edward goes on:

I did not in any way celebrate VE Day. What was the point? Poland – and my people – was not free. Poland had already been taken by Russia. It had not been liberated like many of the Western European nations had. It had been taken, purely because of its position between Russia and Germany. The Yalta Agreement had done nothing to protect us from that, dragging us from one occupier to another occupier, with no respite between them. We then had to wait about fifty years for that occupation to come to an end so that we could have a properly elected leader of our own.

For Poland to have its own democratically elected leader was part of the Yalta Agreement. Or at least it was part of the British and American understanding. The Russians clearly had other motives. The delicate political situation and turmoil in Eastern Europe made interference very difficult.

There is absolutely no doubt that Poland suffered tremendously under German rule. The large concentration of Jews was, as we have seen, the primary target. No known Jew was safe. And any non-Jew harbouring a Jew or restricting the authority's access to Jews, was also marked and arrested. Many of these people found themselves living out their final days before execution in concentration camps. The luckier victims never even reached the camps. We say 'luckier' in its broadest sense. For example, on one occasion, several Polish citizens were shot for helping a small number of Jews evade capture. The Jews themselves were then rounded up and also executed.

A variety of laws were placed on the Polish people, many of which were completely ridiculous. The New Order in Poland laid out ten vital points. These included a provision for German citizens to be served in shops before Poles or anyone else. There was also a demand that the streets should belong to the Germans, and that the pavements were to be kept clear for Germans to use.

Also, Polish males wearing hats were expected to tip those hats when passing important personalities of State and members of the German armed forces. This in itself would create huge resentment. Imagine having to display respect and honour to a member of an organization who that morning may have murdered someone in your family, then being pushed aside because you have no right to the pavement or street.

Poles were also forbidden from using the *'Heil Hitler'* greeting – as if they would wish to use it anyway.

The declaration went on to state that 'Whoever annoys or speaks to German women and girls will receive exemplary punishment. Polish females who speak to or annoy German nationals will be sent to brothels.'

121

Up until the invasion and all the changes that were about to take place, many Poles had been living their lives in reasonable contentment. They were growing up, meeting friends, falling in love, getting married and having children. Michoalina Cichowicz had been born in 1914. She was living in Lwow in Poland when Germany invaded.

> I was due to get married in September 1939 but Hitler had other plans for my future. His troops invaded my country in the same week that my wedding was planned for. Naturally, that event stopped my wedding. I called the invasion a present from Hitler.
>
> I moved away, intent on joining the Polish army. I didn't actually make it at first. I was trapped and sent to prison. It was a Russian prison – yes Russian. The Russians occupied that area at the time. Then I was sent to a camp in Kazakhstan, which was then part of Russia. I was able to get out of there during a special amnesty and finally managed to join the Polish Army. The main group of the army was based in France.

Apart from her stint in the Russian prison Michoalina seemed to have been relatively fortunate. She was able to evade any number of fates that could have descended upon her. She could have been murdered. She could have found herself in any one of a number of concentration camps to work until she dropped. Or she could have been sent for experimentation; a fate which rarely resulted in survival. She continued her story:

> In 1945 I was in Florence, south-west of Bordeaux in France. I was staying with my fiancé. I remember that one of the many things that was scarce during the war were rolls of toilet paper. They were so scarce they were like gold. Suddenly, on VE Day, the rolls were everywhere. They were all in the streets and were being thrown around and being used as if they were streamers. Everyone was so happy. But I was very cautious and concerned about what was going to happen in Poland.

What did VE Day mean for me? It meant very little. It was the end of the war in Europe. And for everyone that was wonderful. But for Poland? No. The Russian occupation went on for far longer than the war. During the war, we were controlled by Germany and we had to say and do what Hitler decreed. Then, later, it was the Russians and we could say and do only what they wanted.

I get sick when I look at a picture of Churchill, Roosevelt and Stalin when they made the agreement of what to do with each territory after the war. I know Poland was in the wrong place, being between Russia and Germany, but it really didn't come out of the agreement very well. I have nothing against Churchill. He wanted what was best for Britain, naturally. But we had so many years after the end of the war to endure under new occupiers.

During the war there were other fates awaiting some females. Each person who survived the initial assault on their lives by trigger happy SS officers or budding pyromaniacs had to contend with uncertain futures. Many of the females were screened. Those of good stock were transported to human stud farms. These were known as *Lebensborn* facilities and were the brainchild of Heinrich Himmler. Just how many girls and women, both German and non-German, were used in this way will probably never be known. Girls were selected for their supposed purity and 'encouraged' to enter into sexual relationships with SS men. Their children would be taken away and raised in special maternity homes. There, they would become the beginnings of the superior race needed to sustain the Thousand Year Reich.

On Polish Independence Day 1939, the Poles were forced to endure further humiliation. Their country had been subjected to over two months of brutal occupation. Their capital, Warsaw, had been relegated to the status of little more than an insignificant town. The men, women and children were virtually starving and had no idea what their futures would be like. That was assuming their rulers allowed them the luxury of having a future at all.

In Lodz, German soldiers marched past a pile of rubble. Two days earlier, the rubble had been the statue of Kosciuszko, a Polish hero. Poles had been ordered to smash it but had been unable. Explosives had achieved the task. On that same day, to commemorate such an occasion, 350 Poles were herded into a yard and forced to dig holes. In small groups, they were shot and the bodies flung into the holes they had just dug.

This was actually quite common during the Second World War, in both Europe and the Far East. It was employed as a method of demoralizing and subjugating an already defeated population. It was employed by conquerors who had little or no regard for the lives of anyone other than themselves. It was used by groups of people who saw themselves as infinitely superior to the people they were victimizing. The victims were seen as sub-human.

The next Pole to relay her experiences was not actually in Poland during the Second World War. Pelangie Throjanowska was nineteen when the German military forces invaded her native country. At the time, she was working as a domestic cleaner and home help in Northern France.

> I was born in Germany. At the time, Poland was divided up, part belonging to Russia, part Prussia. My grandfather had moved to Germany to work in the mines and my parents followed to work in the fields. I was born into a family with twelve children and when I was just two months old, we all moved to France.
>
> We heard about the invasion of Poland over the radio. It was a huge shock. People just couldn't believe it. And the invasion of France took me directly into the war. The troops could often be heard in the town centres, singing various German songs as they exercised. The French people didn't like that and neither did the Polish community. It was terrible, a really frightening time. You always had to be careful of what you did and said in case you vanished into a camp of some sort. And that did happen a lot. From one day to the next, we just didn't know what was happening.
>
> I was living in a mining town throughout the war. Towards the end, as the Allies appeared, the retreating Germans were trying to destroy the mines. I think this was so that the Allies

would find it difficult to use the minerals for their war effort. I had a friend who went shopping one day, leaving her husband and children at home. When she returned, there was no husband, no children, no house. The area had been destroyed by the Germans.

Then one day, I could hear a really loud toot tooting noise coming from one of the trains. It went on and on and when I asked what was going on, someone told me, 'It's all over. The war is over.'

Everyone was celebrating. There were a lot of parties and people were dancing in the streets. I also remember a special church service that day when we all prayed that the peace would last.

Chapter Nineteen

The Children's War

Mavis Dow was eleven years old when Victory in Europe was announced. She had spent the war years in the heavily bombed south-east London suburb of Plumstead, a stone's throw from the Woolwich Royal Arsenal and the River Thames, both major targets for the Luftwaffe. Mavis explained that one night she was invited to stay in a friend's air raid shelter but her mother refused, favouring the communal shelter on Plumstead Common instead. This proved to be a wise decision, as Mavis later discovered that her friend and friend's family were killed by a direct hit from a V1 rocket that very night. Mavis was bombed out of her house and was taken in – with her parents – by a kind man she referred to as 'Uncle Dick'. It was Uncle Dick's daughter-in-law who took Mavis to London on VE day.

> I remember it being a very spontaneous thing. I was told 'come on, we're going to London' and off we went. People just naturally went to London, converging on Trafalgar Square and Buckingham Palace. The whole place was jam-packed with people and I remember being very frightened by the amount of people. There was relief in the air. People were singing songs like *When The Lights Go On*, which was quite famous and oddly, written by a man who my late husband Ian went to school with.
>
> I suppose I haven't seen the Buckingham Palace area so full of people since VE Day, perhaps with the exception of the

Golden Jubilee. I remember the King and Royal Family coming out onto the balcony and that was it really. It was a communal thing, with little structure, just a great sense of relief. People wanted to express that, so they naturally went to Buckingham Palace.

It was late in the day when we went to London but was very late – very dark – when we returned. The whole experience is something that has stayed with me all my life. I would like to think that nowadays one doesn't have to look up at the sky searching for enemy planes, like we did during the Second World War. But what with September 11 there is uncertainty again, and this time, unlike even the Cold War, you have people who are prepared to commit suicide in order to carry out terrorist attacks.

Ron Clayton was a young child during the Second World War, having been born in 1937. He spent some of the war years as an evacuee. Ron's experience of evacuation was not a happy one.

'I spent much of the war in Croydon but was evacuated twice, both times to Nottinghamshire. The first time was during the Blitz and the second was when the doodlebugs were falling. I stayed with friends of my uncle. They ran a pub but of course I was too young to appreciate that luxury. One of my favourite past-times there was fishing.

We were in a very rural area so there were very few bombing raids. There were a few aircraft occasionally passing over on their way to or from towns. I was there with my mother and aunt as my father and uncle were both serving in the forces. I hardly saw them at all.

We were totally unwelcome where we were evacuated to. I was occupying a place in the local school and we became known as bomb dodgers. The locals called us that despite not being on the receiving end of bombing raids themselves. They managed to make us feel extremely out of place and un-popular. Even many years after the war, when we went back to visit, the people who were there during the war did not want to know us nor have anything to do with us.

Once back home in the Croydon area, I remember on one occasion my father and uncle were home on leave. They were both drinking at the local pub when my father realized he had left his cigarettes at home. Because they were in short supply and he would have difficulty getting another packet, he decided to fetch them from home. When he returned to the pub, the pub had been reduced to a pile of rubble by a bomb, killing his brother.

Children tend to make what they can out of any situation with little regard for the consequences. There was one time when a doodlebug fell near home and demolished a few houses. Luckily, everyone was out so there were no human casualties. But it made rather a mess of the houses and we kids had a new adventure playground to play on. We never thought about the dangers. It was exciting.

Some Americans moved in to secure one bombsite and the local children used to congregate around the troops, expecting food. We used to get food from them that we had never seen before, but that didn't always stop us eating it. In fact, we felt more welcome with the Americans who were only there temporarily than we did with the villagers when we were evacuated.

Both my mother and my aunt worked for much of the war years in the local factory, making munitions. That was something they had to do. They needed the money and the war effort needed them.

On both VE Day and VJ Day, we held street parties. The VE Day party was very much a make do affair. I was a little too young to be worried about catering arrangements but there were the problems of rations and lack of time to prepare. It was just a really exciting and happy time. If there were problems with making arrangements, people were happy with having an easier problem like that to surmount than all the other problems we'd been facing for years beforehand.

There were mainly women and children at the party. A few older men were there, but the majority of the younger men were still overseas. My father did not demob until a couple of months after the end of the European war. He was, I think, still in Italy on VE Day. So the women were left to ensure that the children enjoyed themselves as much as possible.

My father had managed to send a food parcel back from Italy. There were all sorts of fruits in there, some of which I had never seen before. But I managed to enjoy them all. Some children were receiving bananas but refused to eat them because they had no idea what they were. On that day, I was waving my flag and giving the Churchill victory salute.

I think the younger generation today find it difficult to appreciate what that period was all about and what it involved. It's like me reading a book about the Tudors. I can understand it but not fully appreciate it because that period is outside my personal experience. I think that's true to some extent for people today. Reading a history book about the war is not the same as experiencing it. And, of course, everyone's experiences are different anyway. You can talk to a dozen people and get a dozen different stories. One example of the difference between knowledge and experience was in a film I saw recently. It was about the Blitz and in it the children were getting excited about barrage balloons. But we never got excited about them because they were part of everyday life. They were there and you thought nothing of them.

Edna Jones was thirteen when the Second World War ended. She was living in Normington, near Wakefield, in Yorkshire. She recalls one occasion when a German aircraft came down nearby.

I think the pilot must have experienced trouble with his engine. He wasn't shot down. He crashed. We all saw this plane coming down quite close to us. The men went searching for the pilot. I think there was just the one German. They used whatever they could grab to chase him. The women from the town were behind the men, carrying cups of tea. Picture the scene – crashed plane, pilot trying to flee, men of the town chasing, and women with refreshments.

The pilot was found because he was marched off to a prisoner of war camp somewhere. I'm not sure where and I had no further information about him. None of us did. But the thing is that the cups of tea weren't so much for the men searching for him, but for the pilot himself! I think a lot of people were probably like that. He was just one lad, by himself and that's what people did.

Apart from that, some of my time was spent farming. In fact, we had time off school in the autumn so we could help with the crops for the harvest. That way, we could all do our bit for the war effort and my main role was the farming of potatoes. At that time, everybody was out: mums, husbands, children. Kids being kids, we quickly got fed up with picking potatoes so we started playing with them.

My area really didn't get bombed very much. It was quite rural so not really a big target. We used to watch the planes flying over on their way to bomb Leeds. That was a high profile target because that's where a lot of industry was based, especially where weapons were being made. I think that's probably why that plane crashed. It was probably on its way to Leeds.

We were a very close community. Everybody knew everybody else. There was one lad who had been fighting and had gone missing. He'd been missing for a long, long time. We'd all given up hope and so had his parents. On D-Day, we saw a film in the cinema of the landings in France. And there he was, on top of one of the tanks. The cinema had been closed, but when the manager first saw the film, he opened the place for everyone, and especially the parents, to watch. The cheer that went up when everyone saw him was massive. We were all so thrilled.

On VE Day, I was staying with a cousin in Shipley. When we realized what it was, everyone got together and made what food we could. A piano was taken out into the street where the celebrations were taking place. The feature of a small town was that everyone knew everyone. My father had been working away from home a lot. He was in one of the munitions factories in Doncaster and stayed there, in digs, for two weeks, then came home for two days and so on.

Once the war was over, it meant that I would see my father

a lot more. That was great. He had been a builder before the war and of course, there would be plenty of work for him afterwards. It's a shame I wasn't able to take any photos at the time. We did have a camera but taking photos was difficult because film was so scarce. But the street party was great.

Patricia Carvell was twelve years old when war was declared. She was evacuated to Bath where she stayed with the relatives of a friend.

A lot of people didn't have the luxury of staying with someone they knew and could live with without there being too much friction. But I was quite fortunate. I knew what type of people they were and what to expect when I arrived. So, overall, I quite enjoyed it. There were three of us going to the same house and Bath was a really nice area.

At that time, my parents were living in Southwark in London. They were being bombed pretty much all the time. I had plenty of news about what was going on in London. There was a great deal of news coming through and if anyone found out something, news spread pretty fast. That, I think, was all down to the community spirit. Everyone was together. Everyone seemed to know everyone else and be interested in how everyone else was doing.

I went back home to London in 1942. There was still bombing going on but not as fierce. There were still the Z Bombs dropping. They were incendiary bombs, giving a huge flash when they detonated, very hot.

I was carrying on with my studies on VE Day. I know everyone else was having a party but I wanted to study. I wasn't really too concerned about any local celebrations although I'm sure there were some. You see, not everyone was partying. Lots of people were working and some over in the Far East were still fighting. I was studying for what I wanted to do in the future because I could now look forward to a good future.

I don't think there can be much emphasis placed on VE Day after all these years because people tend to forget. It's been a long time and why should people who didn't experience it think much about it? I like remembering. I like thinking about what happened before, and whether I remember a particular event or a certain teacher. But perhaps others don't get the same out of it.

May Phillips was fourteen years old at the start of the Second World War. She remembers history lessons that taught her about the Great War as the most recent big conflict and then suddenly found herself living through an even larger one. Like so many people during the Second World War, she performed more than one duty, despite her age. She was living in and around Glasgow for the entire duration.

My surname then was Pepper, and don't think I didn't get some ribbing about that. I'm sure you can guess the kind of thing.

When the war started, I was working in a printing plant and moved into a scheme called War Work. Quite a few other people around me, mainly women, were drafted into the local munitions factory in Glasgow. I didn't join them, maybe because I was too young. As time went on, I wanted to join the Land Army, but only if I could get to work on a farm near home so I could see my family all the time. That couldn't be guaranteed so I gave the Land Army a miss.

For me, the War Work scheme involved working in a facility that made, believe it or not, strips of silver paper. That was actually quite crucial because thousands at a time were dropped from planes over enemy territory during a bombing raid. That way, the German airwaves would be completely scrambled and it would totally confuse what radar systems they had. Using this meant that fewer of our aircraft could be found and consequently more would return from a mission.

Where I was, there wasn't really very much bombing, certainly compared to other areas. A nearby power station was hit and that caused a lot of problems, but I think that was about it. But I was ready for more and part of what I was doing was to watch for fires. I was part of a team, armed with buckets of sand and placed at strategic points. We weren't supposed to tackle a fire if it was beyond our control – just watch for one and alert others. I was often stationed up on flat rooftops where I could get a reasonable view of other buildings around me.

Of course, the arrival of the end of the war in Europe meant we could stop all that. I could stop making the silver strips for bombing missions. I could stop doing the fire watching, because naturally there would be fewer blazes. We all held parties with what provisions we could get hold of. You see, even though food was pretty scarce and the more exotic food was virtually non-existent, we still managed to scrape by. If one person had something that someone else needed to perhaps bake something for the street, then it would be offered. Even before VE Day, there was a great deal of helping other people, but at least VE Day meant that we could look forward to the time when absolute survival didn't depend on it.

Finally, after so long, we could get so many things that we couldn't get before; things like nylons. When the war was raging, we could only get them by talking sweetly to the American soldiers who were stationed nearby. Now, you can get nylon stockings easily, but then, it was a completely different situation.

It's such a shame, but I don't think the youngsters today are taught much about the war. If they were taught, perhaps they might have a slightly better understanding of what it was all about and how we lived through it. I don't think some of them even know about it, let alone about what it was like. And that really is a shame.

Margaret Cormack was born three quarters of an hour before the announcement was made that war against Germany had been declared. She spent the war years moving a great deal with her parents. Home became Frodsham, St Annes, Warmington and Hunts Cross. In 1943, her father went briefly to Canada and she lived with her grandparents. She attended four schools by the age of nine and recalls the gas masks used by virtually the entire population as reminding her of the smell of a dentist's surgery at the time. The family shelter was in the house under the stairs.

I don't really remember much about VE Day. I was only a child. My parents and I were living in Hunts Cross, a suburb of Liverpool, at the time. My most vivid memory was of my father telling my mother, while she was hanging up the flags and bunting, that he was being sent to Europe. He was going to Europe just as other people, previously sent there to fight, might have been thinking about returning home. He was in a reserved occupation, which meant that he was not called up to fight. He worked for the chemical company ICI and was seconded to the Ministry of Supply. The Government needed to know whether there was any evidence of the Germans using mustard gas and my father was a good choice.

He was travelling under the auspices of the American Army and had to wear a military uniform. He had been issued with a tin helmet and a crown and pip to denote his honorary rank of lieutenant colonel. Neither he nor my mother had any idea which way to sew the pip on. Everything was so rushed that she was compelled to give him a needle and thread so he could complete the task himself while he was on the train, bound for London.

I recall VJ Day with more clarity. I was allowed to stay up late. I don't think there is much emphasis placed on either of these important days anymore. We had the fiftieth anniversary of VE Day and that was great but it should be remembered more. The younger generation really don't have any idea of what life was like.

Brian Eccleshall was six years old when the Second World War started. He was living in Upnately, near Basingstoke in Hampshire. He had been born prematurely and was very unwell for much of his first few years. He was taken to the countryside in the hope that he might live perhaps until he was seven.

First of all, we lived in a shack, built by my aunt's husband. Living conditions were very basic. We milked the goats, had a toilet in the middle of a field and drank water from a well. There was no power for lighting except paraffin lamps. It was a little like the Middle Ages – when it gets dark, you go to bed. Transport was not very frequent either. We had two buses each day – one going into Basingstoke and one coming out of Basingstoke. Once a week, we had a van arriving with supplies. That was in the summer. In the winter, we were virtually cut off.

When the soldiers were evacuated from Dunkirk, a lot of the trains travelled through Basingstoke, carrying the troops. My mother was there, giving them cups of tea and she actually saw her brother amongst them. All he had on was trousers and a pair of plimsolls. No shirt. That was how he got out.

There were quite a few American and Canadian troops in the area and all us kids used to go around to their camps and, for some treats, offer to light their fires. More often than not, we didn't because they were concerned we might burn ourselves, but we still managed to get the treats, like chewing gum and sugar. We'd say 'Light your fire, Yank' in much the same vein as children nowadays say 'Penny for the Guy' in November.

When we moved into a house, we had quite a lot of soldiers billeted with us. There were no evacuated children but plenty of troops. Children were evacuated to nearby houses though and the entire programme caused something of a logistical problem for local schools. The original local children attending school in the morning and the evacuees attending in the afternoon overcame that, to some extent. This way, everyone at least received some education, albeit half of what they would otherwise have got, had there not been a war. It was school by shift work.

During the first days of the war, we entertained ourselves as best we could and kids being kids, we didn't always select the most appropriate form of entertainment. A couple of friends and I used to venture down to the Basingstoke Canal where there were always a lot of grass snakes. We would catch a snake, kill it and then chase the girls with it. I doubt

135

whether they appreciated that, but we certainly appreciated the screaming. It was great fun.

During the summer holidays, all us kids would be collected from home and taken, clutching jam sandwiches and a bottle of either cold tea or water, to the fields. There, we would spend entire days either planting or picking, depending on what needed doing at the time. That was our bit for the war effort. Sometimes though, there was a problem. The sewage troughs would be opened and the sewage would flood the fields. It served as manure but occasionally you would pick up what you thought was a potato and it wasn't. Sometimes that happened even before I'd eaten my jam sandwiches and where can you wash your hands in the middle of a field?

Towards the end of the war, my father was transferred back to London. He wanted me to travel with him for the sake of my education. I spent much of the time studying, trying to catch up, so socializing was secondary. One night, a bombing raid hit some houses along the road, killing, amongst others, a couple of my school friends. I was staying that night at my grandfather's house and a lump of shrapnel from the explosion went straight through the bed I would have been sleeping in had I been at home that night.

Coal was very much at a premium. Most of what was being extracted was being used by the military. When a house got completely destroyed by a bomb, we would go scavenging for what we could, especially lumps of coal. It was not very nice to steal under those circumstances, but if we didn't, someone else would. I prefer the term 'liberating' the coal rather than stealing it. That reminds me of films we saw after the war of German children doing exactly the same thing in their country.

I remember we often had mobile ack-ack guns in the area. When enemy planes were flying overhead, the gun crews would stop and set up. If that happened to be outside your home, you soon knew about it. Many homes had their windows smashed not by bombs exploding but by these guns firing.

One of the features with the doodlebugs was the engine

noise. If the engine stopped directly above you, you were probably going to be okay because forward momentum of the flight pattern would carry it away from you. But if it stopped elsewhere, you would be very apprehensive.

I was in Brixton when the war finally came to an end. On VE Day itself, everybody in my local area went absolutely berserk. My house was one of those where the street door opens straight onto the pavement. There was no driveway and no front garden. In the middle of the road was a manhole, which was used as a makeshift wicket for our games of cricket.

On that night, everything seemed to happen. There was a bonfire put over the manhole. I don't know whether it was a gas or water hole. Anyway, everybody was bringing all their rubbish out and throwing it on the fire. Everybody was singing whatever they felt like singing. There was a pub up the road, I think called the Windmill, and as far as I can remember, all the adults were in and out of this place all night long. They were cheering and shouting. Later, on VJ Day, we had the same thing all over again.

A street party was arranged afterwards. I can remember all the mums pooling their coupons for whatever they could get so the children could have a fun time. The problem for major celebrations at the time was that food was difficult to obtain. There was, though, a very communal atmosphere. People were in and out of each other's houses throughout the war years and that was very much a feature of VE Day. Mini celebrations took place inside houses.

'The day meant the end of the bombing, the end of the uncertainty that someone you met today might have been killed by a direct hit tomorrow. But for me, memories of life prior to the war were few and far between. I was only young and couldn't really remember much before it all started. So it was, I suppose, something like a perpetual war to me. I didn't really know any different. The true meaning behind the celebration was probably a little lost on me. But I did enjoy the fact that I could finally stay up late.

I don't recall many streetlights suddenly glowing because

they had all been blackened during the war to protect against bombing raids. Perhaps there were some more than normal – normal to me then – but it wasn't something that struck me as memorable.

I think a few young people have some interest in VE Day, but they are definitely in the minority. We remember it so it means a lot more to us. But I think even people of that era will only tend to remember the good parts and try to blot out the bad parts as much as possible. Some of the bad parts are still in the memory – of course they are – but not with the same emphasis placed on them.

Edward Kindler was nine years old when the war began and was one of the many children to be evacuated.

Being evacuated was a great adventure for me. I was sent to a big house in the countryside. I used to live in London and was sent away with the rest of the school. We lined up with our gas masks and little boxes with labels on at the railway station and off we all went. I went to Leatherhead in Surrey. We had a few belongings, whatever we could carry.

I was one of three children in my family and I reckon my parents probably enjoyed the rest. They had got rid of me for a while. They ran a greengrocer's back home. I stayed where I was for quite a while before returning to London in plenty of time for the end of the war.

I know quite a few people had bad experiences with the evacuation programme that took place. A lot depended on the sort of family you were billeted with, and the area. Schooling was an interesting situation. Because there were extra students in certain areas that had not had them before, some went to class in the morning and some in the afternoon. It was like schooling on shift work. Otherwise, those schools would have been terribly overcrowded.

Towards the end of the war, when the doodlebugs started, I think I found that quite exciting. We had no idea where they would strike and I used to go clambering over the wreckage sites – you know, doing my bit to help clear up.

On VE Day, I remember going to Lambeth and watching from Lambeth Bridge some of the celebrations. I was by myself and trying to get a good vantage point. Unlike a lot of the people around me, I didn't drink any alcohol. I was only about fourteen. You wouldn't believe the crowds. There were fireworks and searchlights. But for a change, the searchlights were sweeping the sky as part of the celebrations, not looking for enemy planes as they had for so many years. That was one of the great things about it really. Searchlights were no longer being used to hunt for aircraft that might drop bombs.

It was a time of mixed emotions because many people had lost someone they cared about. I had lost a couple of distant uncles but no one really close. Apart from that, I think we were quite lucky, although most of the family were in London and being bombed.

The whole experience, I think, has now all been forgotten. Nobody takes any notice anymore. It's all dead and buried until you get someone asking for information. I think that some of those people who lost loved ones in the war might probably rather forget about it.

Winifred Lankford, who was evacuated from Glasgow during the war, has now made a new life for herself in Australia.

I was evacuated to Aberfeldy, in Scotland. That was in 1940, when I was twelve and I absolutely hated every minute of it. The place I ended up in was really not very pleasant. I think I was completely the wrong age for evacuation and was basically tolerated by the family I was staying with. I was under the care of a barber and his pregnant wife and really resented having been sent away. I had a family back home and felt that if I was going to die, I would rather die with my loving family than with a couple who neither wanted me nor cared about me. I was being treated like a housemaid. Having come from a home where I was the youngest girl, I had been a bit spoilt. I had no idea what to do with a broom.

There was a supervisor – not really a supervisor but that's the closest term for it – whom we could approach if we were being unfairly treated or if the people we were with were being cruel. But what good would that have done? I probably would have been shifted elsewhere and what I really wanted was to go home.

When I finally did return to my family in Glasgow, my mother made a comment that has remained with me ever since. She told me that I looked so countrified, moments before she laughed. What a sensational greeting.

When the end of the war in Europe was announced, I was in a theatre. The play stopped for a moment for an important announcement and the place just erupted into absolute rapture. It was so euphoric. That pause in the play went on and the show was never actually finished that day. What was the point? No one would have been interested in a play anymore when we had just emerged from half a decade of war on our doorsteps.

For me, at least my brother would be safe. His name was Jack and he was a navigator in the Royal Air Force, flying usually in bombers. And we had a neighbour who had been serving since he was fifteen in the Merchant Navy, mainly on the Russian and Atlantic convoys. I also had an American cousin who had been able to supply us with luxuries such as chewing gum and nylons. He had been born in Scotland and then moved to America. When he returned with his battalion on draft, he found himself back in the same town as he had been born in. How's that for a coincidence?

There was still a lot of concern for quite a large amount of people. Japan was still fighting and many people knew someone who was involved in that conflict, so far from home. I think, once VJ Day arrived, we were still euphoric from the effect of VE Day and it was more of a continuation of the same celebration, three months later.

I think it would be impossible for us to fight another war like that. Warfare isn't the same anymore, but if it were, there is so little comradeship now that it would be quite impossible for people to pull together and be so willing to help others. I doubt whether they would be able to cope with the hardships and the constant bombings. Glasgow wasn't as badly hit as other areas, like London. Those in London really put up with so much and were wonderful.

James Bause was just nine years old at the end of the war. He recalls the Battle of Britain very well.

The Battle of Britain, I recall, was fought mostly over Kent. Naturally, quite a lot of the aircraft had to fly over Kent to reach London and by the time some of the enemy planes reached London, our pilots were well engaged against them and we really did a good job on them. Quite a few came down near Egerton, where I lived. I can remember seeing farmers marching German pilots to the local police station to be dealt with.

When the action grew more intense, my father changed his job to become a sand and ballast truck driver. He was involved in the construction of Stanstead Airport. This was being built by the American Air Force to operate B-17 Flying Fortress bombers. He made the journey four times a day.

Being so young at the time, I think I found the whole situation quite exciting. There was a rail line nearby and it was used for a locomotive pulling an AA Gun. Every time it fired, the gun moved along the line and had to be repositioned. The noise was incredible.

On one occasion, our neighbour had an incendiary bomb drop through his upstairs bedroom ceiling. He picked it up with a shovel and put it out the window, setting the curtains alight in the process. The ARP told us that sometimes these bombs were filled with sand by the Polish labourers forced to make them, to limit the damage.

When the V2 rockets started, one of the first dropped nearby. The blast rushed along an alley and demolished much of the front of the house. We even had to accommodate one of the bomb damage people who came to help us because many of them came from the north.

Although there were horrendous moments, like when an air raid shelter in Crystal Palace, full of people, took a direct hit or when a woman was killed in her bedroom by a low flying plane shooting through roof tops, or a flying bomb killing sixty people in a pub, there were some more humorous occurrences. I remember the hilarity when a barrage balloon fell into our school. That was great.

Being young, I had a really great time on VE Day. There was a terrific celebration. The pavement of our street was filled with rows of tables and several streets converged on the one. Everything kicked off at about lunch time, as I recall, and went on for the rest of the day. There were games in the afternoon and then a small band got together and played through much of the evening. I think it probably goes without saying that, for many, the alcohol flowed. Then we did it all over again on VJ Day, although that was more of a grown-up event and focused even more on alcohol. The pub did a good trade.

I saw a great deal of fun and excitement during the whole event. I was young and I think at that age, you probably look at most things as being fun. I think youngsters now, who would not have any personal experience of the war, would find it very difficult to comprehend what it was all about.

Evelyn Witt was eight years old on VE Day. She spent the war years at home with her family while attending school in Bromley. Her father had served in the First World War and was in the Home Guard in the Second World War. Having also worked as a foreman for the Gas Board, he was ideally qualified to check for leaks of gas after bombing raids.

VE Day was a very significant day. It meant the end of all the bombing. It meant we could eat meals in peace without having to run to the shelters, it meant you could close your door without risk of it being blasted off its hinges and it meant an end to the threat of evacuation for children. It also meant I could try new foods I had never tasted before because of the rations and lack of all the exotic foods we take for granted now. And it also meant the end of nightly blackouts.

I was never evacuated during the war. It was a joint family decision that we would stay together regardless and my sister, being eleven years older than me, was beyond the evacuation age anyway. My parents were not keen on children growing up away from home and of course at the time, no one knew how long it was going to last. It could have been years. When we did go away to try to escape the bombing for a while, it was with us all together. The bombing was intense, especially during the night and it was worse before the doodlebugs. When they started, you tended to become a bit blasé about them. As long as the engine didn't stop above you, you were okay. But sometimes, they did fly back. They seemed to turn, whether it was the wind or some mechanism inside them, like a gyro, but something often made them turn mid flight and come back again.

I remember once there was a direct hit on a shelter in Lewisham. Just behind where the market is now, there was then a shelter full of people. A bomb hit it and the bodies, I believe, were just left until later. There would have been no survivors. Shelters could protect against blasts some way off, but not direct hits. The only shelters that were likely to withstand heavy blasts were those that nature had created for us. Chislehurst Caves was used as a shelter. You paid for your space and often left bits and pieces in there during the day. Nothing ever got stolen. There was even a hospital and theatre in there. Being inside a hill, it was a natural protection for the people inside.

Our own shelter was a hole in the ground. My father added an angled entrance so a blast ripping the door off wouldn't catch us inside. Over the hole was a metal roof. It was always wet inside and sometimes, when the sirens sounded; we had to run along the garden to the shelter. If we were eating dinner, take the plate with you, making sure you didn't spill any potatoes as they rolled around on the plate. And the gravy. My mother made for me a special all in one suit that was like a boiler suit but with buttons in the right places for necessary functions without needing to remove the suit. It was called a siren suit.

Sometimes, though, we didn't bother to go into the shelter. We had a billiard table in one room that some of the RAF personnel from Biggin Hill nearby played on. It was really sturdy and we used to all hide under there during some of the air raids.

We often left the front door unlocked and the windows open, without any worry of people stealing our possessions. Mind you, if you didn't do that, you might lose your door or windows when a bomb exploded nearby. Leave the door open and you'll at least have a door to close later. There was one chap who was completely deaf and so he couldn't hear the siren. He shut his front door when he went into the house and was walking upstairs when a bomb blast smashed the door up the stairs after him. I don't think he knew what had hit him.

One place I remember seeing hit was a cemetery in Bromley. It had three direct bombing raids in one night. You can imagine what it must have been like – body parts scattered everywhere and the smell was appalling. But people shrugged and thought – well, they're dead anyway.

There were always air battles going on overhead and when the doodlebugs arrived, Bromley was one of the areas over which planes stopped chasing them. What the RAF used to do was try to flip a V1 off course with its own wing. But if the rocket had reached as far as Bromley, everywhere beyond towards London was fairly heavily populated. So the flying bombs would kill someone after that so the pilots had to let them go. Bromley was one of the last opportunities to knock a V1 down. Rather than bring all of them down on Bromley, they used to let them go.

One day, when the Battle of Britain was on, I was on a train and we pulled into a siding. Above us were the dogfights. I was young so it didn't really occur to me how terrible it could have been but I found it absolutely fascinating. I hung out of the window of the train, watching planes zipping around amongst each other, fighting in very close quarters.

I was machine-gunned once. I will never forget that. I had stayed late at school because I was the board monitor. I had to clean the black board. There were two fields, separated by a road, which I had to go across. Above one field was a barrage balloon with some ATS girls looking after it. I looked to my left and there was a plane coming across the field towards the road. It was very low; too low. The pilot was machine-gunning, ripping the road up. I can still see his face. I froze and the boy with me froze. I remember thinking that the boy is going to get really told off because the shots ripped the pocket off his clothes. It was that close. It's a child type of logic that thinks of someone getting told off for losing a pocket and ignoring the real potential loss.

I think the pilot was aiming for the barrage balloon. That went up in flames, and I'm sure some of the ATS girls were killed. I started to scream and run. The pilot turned around to have another go. My father saved my life. He grabbed the boy and me and flung us to the ground, lying on top of us. I understand that this was the first incident of the Luftwaffe clearing the way for the bombing raids on Lewisham. The fighters were getting rid of the barrage balloons to clear the way for the bombers.

It's amazing how fortunes can favour some and not others. We were very lucky with bombing raids. No houses on our road were flattened, yet several on the next street were. On one occasion, there was black smoke coming from the kitchen and my father thought we had been hit. We all ran from the shelter, only to discover that my mother had left the suet pudding on. I can't tell you what he called her.

We had advance warning of all air raids. Even before the sirens, our cat used to hide under a copper boiler in the kitchen. When the cat vanished under there, we had about two minutes before the sirens would sound. So we had plenty of time to get to the shelter. Who needed air raid warnings when you have a cat? I hope we will never hear the air raid warning sound again – the up and down wailing noise – because it would bring back too many memories for too many people. But, of course, with our cat, we didn't need it anyway.

Everyone was issued with gas masks in cardboard boxes because the authorities were convinced we would be gassed. 'Never forget your gas mask,' I was always told. But it never happened. I think the Germans probably realized that we had gas weapons as well and if they used them, we would use them. They cancelled each other out, like nuclear weapons today. But at least the precaution had been taken.

Darkness was a key issue. No one could put on any lights in their houses until they had closed their curtains completely and then only if the curtains were thick enough to block the light. Home guard patrols could often be heard calling 'Put that light out'. Windows of trams and buses were covered in sticky tape to stop windows blasting in and smothering passengers with smashed glass and there were no lights inside the vehicles. My father's bike had a light on it with the top blacked out so the light only shone downwards.

On VE Day, I was given a banana. I had never seen a banana before and had no idea what to do with it. 'It's fruit', my father told me. Still not sure, I assumed it must be like an apple. I knew what they were like to eat so I ate it like an apple, skin included. Straight in, bite, chew and yuk. And banana skin is very bitter. I didn't know, but I knew I didn't like it very much. Goodness knows what I would have done with a pineapple or a coconut.

I spent the day attending a street party that my father had organized. It was a huge party and he had somehow managed to obtain a large tub of ice cream. That went down a treat with us kids. We hadn't had ice cream for quite a while and some had never had any at all. I still have the bell that he rang to call everyone out for the party. It's an old school bell and it means so much to me. The bell meant VE Day.

So everything outside was decked out in red, white and blue. Someone had dragged a Joanna – a piano – out into the street. There were no curtains pulled across and we had as many lights glowing as we could possibly find. That evening, I went up Bromley Hill and waited for the streetlights to come on. Up until then, I had never seen the streetlights on. And the cheer that went up when they came on was wonderful. It was like freedom. It was better than the Christmas lights in Oxford Street because we had endured about five years of walking around in virtual darkness. Then suddenly everything was lit.

It was like every birthday party rolled into one. We had cakes and ice cream. It was the end of what to me was a perpetual war that had lasted all my life. We knew we could even get things like pet food. We once had budgerigars in an aviary and my father had one day during the war told me that they had all flown away. In fact, he had been forced to kill them because birdseed was not available.

Another great feeling was that we knew that finally we could go to another town, read a signpost that told us to go one way and actually find the town in that direction. During the war all the direction signs had been turned around to confuse any invading German troops.

When the rations were on during the war, I never had sweets. The sugar coupons my mother had were used for obtaining actual sugar for baking cakes, not for treats. So to suddenly stand in a queue to get some sweets was wonderful to a child of the time.

It was also great to know we didn't have to recycle tea. During the war, after we had drunk our tea, I had to spread the used tea leaves out onto a baking tray so they could be dried in the oven for re-use. Four teaspoons instead of two made another cuppa. I was no longer the tea girl of the family.

I was a bit bemused at first by all the fun and jollity. My life had involved war and darkness at night and bombs falling and suddenly that was all over. It was a little while before I could come to terms with it all and fully appreciate what everyone around me was really celebrating.

In one respect, VE Day was spent laughing one minute and crying and reflecting the next. My sister's fiancé was still in Burma, fighting against Japan. There was then no sign of him coming home. Her mind was elsewhere. But when he came home, we had another celebration around VJ Day. Even though the war was still going on, VE Day was so special. It was the end of our war because Japan wasn't dropping bombs on Britain.

I think that all that happened at that time should be remembered. Anything that brings it to the forefront is a really good thing and has achieved something worthwhile. People need to be educated on how we lived, how we survived and what we endured. The Imperial War Museum might put on a show – an air raid simulation – but people seeing the show know that, afterwards, they're coming out without a scratch. It's difficult to put someone in the position of sitting in a wet and cold hole in the garden, never knowing whether the next blast would be the last thing you ever hear. And having that most nights.

I don't know whether it sounds silly, but the whole time was also a good experience. Experiencing what we had experienced was a hell of a good grounding for life. To be on that poverty line like that, I could make do. Now, I can make do if I'm short of something, I can improvise far better than I think a lot of people can do in modern times. It was bad for people who lost relatives and friends and bad for people who were in camps and people like that but a good grounding for those of us who were young at the time.

Chapter Twenty

Thanks for the Memories

Former Prime Minister Sir Edward Heath needs little introduction. However, his role during the Second World War and his introduction to the Nazis as early as 1937 has often been overlooked.

In the summer of 1937 my parents agreed to allow me to take part in a student exchange programme with a boy from Düsseldorf. This eventually led to a personal invitation from the German embassy – in London – to attend the forthcoming Nuremberg rallies (between 6-13 September).

You can't take what the press reported in those circumstances as being automatically genuine. There wasn't any paranoia going on in Germany, in fact there was a large degree of support.

The Nuremberg rallies were so massive and so well organized, you recognized for the first time what a fearsome threat Hitler and his forces would be. His main strength was through the power of his speech making. It struck the right chords with the German people. He showed the strength that the people needed, because they felt that they had suffered at the hands of those who drafted the Versailles Treaty, and the weak leaders they had endured during the 1920s and 30s.

When Hitler entered the rally, there was an enormous fanfare. I was sitting on the inside of the walkway leading up to the platform where he was to deliver his speech. It was so narrow that I wondered how Hitler was going to move up it, flanked by his guards. In fact, he walked up alone with guards behind him, and his shoulder brushed mine as he went past.

During the winter of 44-45, I was part of an offensive moving towards Germany. I took part in Operation Veritable, an offensive to capture the land between the Rhine and Maas. My regiment crossed the Rhine at the beginning of April 45. We entered German territory for the first time during the night of the 5th at Marienbaum, north-west of Essen. I celebrated VE Day on 8 May with my battery, in the region of Kleve. The war had ended, but our work was far from over. We then started a battlefield-clearance operation of the area west of the Rhine, and at the end of May, we moved on to Hanover as part of the occupying force there. We took over a modern sanatorium, which was empty. At last my battery could enjoy some comfort.

Florence Sarah Gatling had a marriage connection to military history. Her husband's great-grandfather was the inventor of the famous Gatling Gun. She was thirty-one years old on VE Day.

I was living in Hampstead at the start of the war. My husband was called into the police. He couldn't get into the armed forces because he was suffering from kidney problems. I had a son of eight who was evacuated to live with relatives in Somerset. He really didn't like it so he came home after a very short while.

I used to go out at night, doing night watching. I was one of the public acting as advance warning for other areas. It was my duty to look for enemy aircraft, including the doodlebugs. When those awful flying bombs appeared, I remember there was a lot of panic. We had no real idea what they were and what was happening. One woman was panicking so much, I actually had to hit her to shut her up. Then I realized my husband was late home and I thought something had happened to him so I started panicking too. Anything could have happened. But thankfully he had just been delayed by a couple of hours. He then had to hit me to shut me up. I'm not normally a panic prone person, but with bombs falling all the time anywhere and everywhere, you soon change.

Our bomb shelter was under the stairs. They were really sturdy stairs so it seemed an obvious place. We were there quite a lot.

Just before the end of the War, we moved to Shepherd's Bush. My husband had been offered a new job there and it was an ideal opportunity. He would be working as a manager in a shop. That was where we were on VE Day.

I didn't go to any official celebrations on the actual day because I don't think there were any. As far as I was concerned, it was all very low key. We just picked ourselves up from the war and got on with our lives. There was very little more than that. I do know other areas had celebrations, but it all seemed to pass my area by. We were just so grateful it was all over and we could move on.

Thea Stride was twenty-four in 1945. She lived in south-east London throughout the war.

I was living in Catford. Catford wasn't really hit very much, but Lewisham, which is only just down the road, was hit quite a lot. I knew a lot of people who were bombed out of their homes, but I wasn't personally. I was quite fortunate from that point of view.

Even though Catford wasn't really much of a target, we still had to frequently run to the shelters, each time hoping we would have a house to return to afterwards, after we were given the all clear. But even in the shelters, we were not completely safe. They could only protect you from a blast nearby. They would not protect you from a direct hit.

My husband was called up into the Army but he wasn't fighting and didn't have to go overseas. He was serving in Lewisham, nice and close to me.

They were terrible times, but you just had to carry on. I mean, if you didn't just carry on, what could you do? We were rationed and that was tough, but again, there wasn't much choice. You had to make do. You had just the bare minimum to survive.

There were a lot of cases when people I met each day suddenly weren't there one day. They'd taken a direct hit. That happened so often. After a while, you started to accept that this would happen and that some people were gone. So what? You just had to carry on. They were more casualties. It was such a strange, horrible time. I think it was probably the first time our actual homes were threatened by warfare.

On the lead up to the end of the war, we were kept very much in the dark as to what was going on in Europe. Even after the D-Day landings, there were still disasters so they had to be kept quiet. And I suppose the troop movements through Europe had to be kept fairly quiet.

When the war finished in Europe, I was at home. There were lots of local celebrations going on but I wasn't actually involved in any of them. Like many of my neighbours, I opened my front door and let locals wander in and out and we chatted and had a little drink and our own little celebrations virtually on the doorstep. There was such a wonderful community spirit. There had to have been during the war and afterwards, everyone was really friendly and happy. It was often a case of if you could help someone, you would. We had experienced such a communal life for the last five years of war. VE Day was no different from that point of view.

You see, I was quite limited on what I could go to and the sort of celebrations I could attend. My children were only very young so I had to look after them. So street parties in other neighbourhoods and trips elsewhere to celebrate were out of the question for me. And because of the rationing and lack of time to prepare for anything, I think celebrations were limited anyway.

I felt absolutely elated that the fighting in Europe was all over. No one else need die, at least in Europe. It was such a special day. But, as the years have gone by, people don't really seem to have much of an understanding now. It's all very well to hear about it, but unless you've actually experienced it, you won't be able to understand it.

Marjorie Carmichael was living in Belfast at the start of the war. She was nineteen years old and working in a drawing office. She had three brothers, all of whom were less restricted by their parents in their movements than she was, purely because she was a girl. Marjorie tells us that there is one special event in her life she perhaps owes to the war.

I was a tracer in a drawing office, working for a civilian company. What I had to do was wait for special drawings to come in and then I and the other tracers would transpose them onto tracing cloth. The company I worked for – Harland & Wolff – was involved in the construction of ships. Some of them were military ships, smaller military ships usually. But the bulk of its business came from building civilian ships, primarily cargo vessels. I knew that a lot of those ships were destined for the trans-Atlantic convoys.

Belfast suffered from a few severe air raids. I think there were two or three really bad ones. I managed to escape the brunt of the attacks though because I lived in the suburbs and the bombers were mainly targeting the centre of the city. That was where a lot of the factories were.

During the war, I was able to develop a relationship and after a little while, got married. He was an engineering draftsman. He was involved in the shipping business too and that was how we met. I think that, had the war not taken place, I may not have even met him. The war was still going on but life can't be put on hold. We moved to Glasgow, where we stayed until he died. It was tuberculosis that killed him. We had got married during the war and my husband had died during the war.

I was living back on the outskirts of Belfast on VE Day. After my husband died, I moved back there. I was working again in the same drawing office as I had been before. We were all given the day off when peace in Europe finally arrived. There were huge celebrations and parties. It was great to be able to go out at night and see lights on every-where. They had been darkened for so long. The scenes were wonderful. Everyone was out having a sensational time;

everything around was so bright and cheerful. And of course bombs would no longer be dropped.

I remember there were flags flying everywhere. We had a wonderful time, even with the rationing that was still going on. In fact, we didn't even really think of rations. We used what we could and made do. What we were lacking in food and drink, I think we more than made up for in the atmosphere of jollity we were creating for ourselves. I wasn't aware of any open house situations, where people travelled from one house to the next, chatting and drinking, but it must have happened. That was just how friendly everyone was.

'My father was very protective. Even though I had been married, he was still watching over me. He put a curb on me attending any of the main celebrations. It wasn't the celebrations he objected to – far from it. He just didn't want me venturing into the centre of Belfast. 'You never know what happens there,' he used to tell me.

Lilly Pye was thirty-two years old when the Second World War ended. She had spent some of the war years living in Abbey Wood, south-east London and working in a factory, manufacturing wireless components.

I stopped going to work when I fell pregnant. Towards the end of the war, I was evacuated, I think mainly because I was pregnant and a bombing raid near me might have caused all sorts of extra complications. That was when the V1 rockets started appearing. I went to live with relatives in Hampshire. I returned to Abbey Wood once, but the bombing was continuing so I went back to Hampshire. My son was born there and I remained there until the end of the war.

My husband was serving in the Royal Navy. He had previously been working for St John's ambulance brigade so it was a natural transition for him to become a medic in the Navy. He was onboard ship some of the time and the rest of the time he was stationed in Tonbridge. I was always worried about him because I never knew how he was doing and whether he would become a casualty himself.

On VE Day, I was back in Abbey Wood. There were lots of local celebrations during the day. I couldn't really do much because I had a baby to look after. He was, of course, my priority, more important than going to any celebrations. But they were happening all around me all day. During the evening, I certainly remember going to a firework display. I'm not quite sure exactly where it was but it was quite local to home. My mother-in-law looked after my son then.

One of the greatest things about VE Day was not really the celebrations, although what I did see were nice. The most important feature to me was that I could finally bring up my baby in peace. There would be no more falling bombs, no more wondering when I would next see my husband, no more moving around the country unless we wanted to. It was finally a peaceful time and at least children who were only babies then could experience a world free from air raids and great loss. I'm sure many other mothers would have felt much the same. Once they'd had chance to think about the enormity of it all, and once they had calmed down and realized that it was actually all over across Europe, raising children in peaceful circumstances would probably be one of their more over-riding thoughts. You always try to get the best for your children and after all those years of all that uncertainty, peace was one of the best gifts we could give.

Harry Brimble joined the Royal Marines in 1940. He was seventeen years old at the time and overall has fond memories of his service, under the circumstances.

The Royal Marines are now divided into commando units, like 40 Commando, 42 Commando and so on. But that wasn't really the situation during the war. The units were far smaller and didn't have such designations. There were groups then rather than brigades although each small group was part of a larger group.

I was serving mainly at Lympstone in Devon and overseas. The Marines have always been considered a front-line force and in a lot of areas, I was involved in spearheading the advance after D-Day. I was right up there in the thick of it and it was exhilarating but also quite frightening.

I was involved in the back-up part of D-Day. My group didn't land on that specific day, but shortly afterwards, once the beaches had been secured. However, once we had landed, we moved quite swiftly through to our designated areas and found ourselves up at the front. We liberated some areas faster than others as we met different levels of resistance along the way. One day, we would move twenty miles without hardly any problem, another time it would be twenty feet and we would be there all day, fighting to gain the upper hand.

As we were fighting our way across Europe, we encountered some of the V1 and V2 launch sites. Many of these were in the Netherlands. We didn't stay there very long. We operated hit and run raids on the sites – go in, disable the site and get back out before the guards knew what had happened.

I reached the border of Germany by the middle of the advance and was well inside Germany by the end. I then returned to the UK with my group. We were back there, at the barracks, on VE Day. That was in Chatham. The celebrations seemed to be quite low-key and most of us still had plenty of work to do. Troops were still in Europe and they still needed supporting. Although we were in the UK, we had no real idea what was going to happen. We may have been destined to be sent back out to Europe to look after the peace. There might have been something like a political vacuum in Germany and unless you had military forces there to stabilize the situation, it could have been quite dangerous.

Even though a lot of people were celebrating, we were preparing ourselves for the possibility of this new stint in Europe. Luckily, there were no plans for us to be sent out to the Far East to fight against Japan.

Kay Jennings was born in 1922, daughter of a veteran of the First World War, granddaughter of a veteran of the Boer War. She was living in Nottingham when the Second World War started and had just left school. Her husband, who had just returned from Dunkirk when they met, soon left to fight in the Far Eastern campaign. He was an officer in the Army and found himself in India, having left behind a wife and a baby.

We travelled around quite a lot, especially at the beginning of the war. That was before my husband had been posted to India. I had my son, Paul, with me. He was the only one of my children born during the war.

While the war was raging and my husband was away, my son and I lived in quite a large house. There was plenty of room for others, so when the Americans started arriving for the preparations for D-Day, we had a few American officers staying with us. There were men throughout the house, and that must have really confused my son. He had never seen his real father before but there were plenty of other men around. So, when my husband did return home, my son started calling him Uncle Daddy. What a term.

On VE Day, my husband, who had spent most of the war away, came home. His regiment had done some kind of draw. Some members, selected purely at random, were able to return home for the celebrations and my husband was one of those whose ticket was drawn. It was a pure fluke that I actually had my husband with me at that wonderful time, and a very pleasant fluke. It was a special kind of leave – I think called something like the Order of Lear, or something like that. Anyway, I'm sure it must have created some jealousy amongst the others who were not lucky enough to return. It was very much like a lottery and those are always based purely and solely on luck.

The journey home was by sea so the bulk of the two weeks leave they were allowed was travelling time. They must have known in advance that the war in Europe was almost over because with that length of journey, VE Day would have been finished by the time they arrived. So the journey must have started earlier because I know my husband was definitely at home with my son and I on VE Day.

Of course, my husband had not seen his son before and vice versa; hence then, the confusion for the child and the name of Uncle Daddy. But we were able to celebrate as a family unit and that was really very nice. We all had very mixed emotions because of the circumstances. It was a joyous time – true. But also, both my husband and I knew that he was only on leave and would have to go back to his regiment in India very soon afterwards. That meant that we only had a very short space of time to celebrate before he had to return to the fighting.

I think there is still quite a lot of interest in the war and its end, even after all these years. It's a long time – sixty years – but there are still quite a lot of people who want to know about it and about what was going on. This book is such a perfect example of the interest.

Margaret Luckett was twenty-eight when peace came to Europe and VE Day became a reality.

I was a midwife during the war and I was kept busy. Very busy. There were a lot of Canadian soldiers near where I was stationed, which of course always presented a bit of a temptation to the local girls. It was always very foggy and I don't know whether the weather actually had any impact on what was going on. But I guess some of the young women could sneak out and meet their Canadian friends for a secret liaison in the fog.

I was also based for a while in the London Underground. That was used as an air raid shelter, although it had not been planned as such. I think it was probably one of the most famous shelters. Everyone within reasonable distance of a station was allocated to that station. I suppose that prevented too much overcrowding in one place although they were rather crowded.

There were occasions when women would go into labour and we could not move them closer to an ambulance in time. So I was on hand to help with the birth, right there on the underground platform. And some of the people sheltering nearby would often help too, with towels and hot water. A baby's birth certificate could read for instance Liverpool

Street Station as place of birth. It puts new meaning to the phrase 'Mind the gap' doesn't it. Look out, there's not a train coming, there's a baby coming.

Overall, everyone I worked with was very disciplined. I had a really good time, working with a lot of really nice people. That was except perhaps one sister. She always demanded everyone of her staff stand when she entered a room and would often wait outside a room for someone to open the door for her. So we frequently left it a while longer than we could just to keep her waiting a little longer.

I was on duty on VE Day. But I was very aware of some of the celebrations that were taking place around the area. I was in Ashford in Kent and there were quite a few Americans nearby. They descended – en masse – at the nurse's home and sang to us. They seemed quite unprepared to leave, even when the police arrived to see if there was an emergency there. But the singers' efforts were wasted because I think the nurses inside just ignored them.

My brother always wanted to go into the church so it all meant that he could pursue that as a career. The day and what it meant to us all was that we could all get on with what we wanted to do. We could carry on with living our lives in a way that warfare didn't dictate.

Alan Luckett was born at the outbreak of the Great War. When the Second World War started, he was working in a bank. Shortly after, he volunteered to join the armed forces but didn't manage quite what he set out to achieve.

In March 1940, I volunteered to join the Royal Air Force. That was what I really wanted. But the Air Force told me that there was no room for me there so I should go below to the Army. That was what the Air Force thought of the Army. You go below to join the Army. When I got to the recruiting office for the Army, the sergeant there was someone I had been working with at the bank.

I was graded as an A1 soldier and promoted to staff sergeant. I was in the pay corps of the Royal Artillery and destined to remain there because once you got promoted to sergeant, you couldn't transfer out.

I can remember almost single handily halting the Americans on one occasion. There was a group of American soldiers training and practising for the Normandy invasion around the area of Foots Cray in Kent. It was an exercise in preparation for the real thing. I managed to stop them all by throwing clumps of soil and dirt at them. The adjudicators who were overseeing the exercise agreed that the clumps were the equivalent of bombs so I had wiped the Americans out.

When I moved to York, I was first of all tasked with cleaning bikes. I refused and was hauled in to see the brigadier. He agreed that cleaning bikes was a waste of my talents and resources and offered me a promotion to, I think it was major, in the tank corps. But I knew nothing about tanks and felt that because of my lack of knowledge, I could not lead others in a tank. So I was transferred back to Foots Cray and became a physical training instructor. By the end of the war, I had been promoted to Warrant Officer – WO2.

I never became a commissioned officer when I could have been sent to India. Apart from the brief stint in York, I was billeted at home near Foots Cray for the whole of the war. I had two daughters and was able to see them quite a lot. One had been born before the war and the younger was born during the war, just after it had started.

While I was there, the first person I had to drag out of a bombed house was the best friend of my first wife. That made it all very real for me.

On VE Day, I can remember seriously waiting for my discharge. I knew it would come quite soon, although it didn't actually happen until the following January. But once that had happened, I would be able to return to the bank.

I spent the actual day in central London with an ATS girl. She was a lovely girl, really lovely. It was so crowded there you really couldn't see anything properly. The impression I got was that no one really knew what they were doing. VE Day had jumped on us so quickly, we didn't have time to realize the enormity of it all. I don't know whether even

Churchill could have known what was really going on. There had not been the time to plan. And besides, what planning could we do with rations? But I mingled with the crowds and soaked up the atmosphere, with my ATS girl.

I seem to recall having no trouble getting home. I think I was travelling in a virtually empty carriage. Perhaps the trains were travelling out of London at that time to bring people into London for the night time celebrations. I got back at about ten o'clock that evening.

The next day, I think some of the celebrations were still going on. But I had to report back to the mess. Oh and what a mess. The sergeant had let the soldiers have their own celebration there and drink had obviously flowed really well. Everyone had been in there, soldiers, non-commissioned officers, officers, civilians – just about everyone you could possibly think of. And by the end of the war, the mess officer in charge had managed to accumulate so much in tips, he was able to buy three houses. He had been very well organized and he did all right out of the war.

Raymond Baxter OBE is best known for his long-term career as a presenter of BBC1's *Tomorrow's World* programme. He has always loved technology and above all aircraft. His commentary for many televised air shows is widely appreciated, but not so well known is his often-covert operations as a Spitfire pilot during the Second World War. He was a flight lieutenant during Operation Big Ben – the dive-bombing Spitfire missions.

We had Spitfire IXs for standing patrol over Arnhem. Pretty ineffective because the weather was so bad. We were then withdrawn to Coltishall. So we were pulled out of the front line. We were furious about that but were soon told that we were to be re-equipped with clipped wing Spitfire XVIs. I loved that aeroplane from the word go. We were told about the mission that would become known as Operation Big Ben and we would be teamed with 453 Squadron (Australian) and 603 Squadron. We worked out of Coltishall to begin with.

Every now and again we were affected by bad weather but

161

that was the exception rather than the rule, because you see Maxie Sutherland would fly round and round and wait for a hole in the cloud, then dive-bomb. We were very determined.

We never dive-bombed at night. Total waste of time and extremely dangerous. It was a close formation exercise and we bombed in sections of four. And if you were leading, you flew over the target, and you would round your wing and count two and roll on your back and come down like that. And every aeroplane would do the same thing. So, ideally, it was a stream of four aeroplanes very close together. And you bombed individually, but obviously, you didn't drop your bomb until the leader pulled away. And that was the trick to make it successful. It all depended, to a considerable extent, on how good the leader was. Because if he was too far away and his dive wasn't steep enough, then the other dives would tend to be flatter and flatter, which was dangerous.

On one occasion, I looked in my mirror, and one chap was pulling out. This was my number two. He was pulling out before I dropped my load. So I posted him. He never flew with us again.

The dive itself was always 70 to 75 degrees. Ideally, you would start at 8,000 feet, drop the bomb at 3,000 feet and pull out.

The Germans originally released their V2s from a suburb in the Hague – the corner of a street – but they gave that up. I knew that part of Holland like the back of my hand. We studied the maps very carefully, and actually, one target, the oxygen plant, which we called the 'Winegar Works', was actually in a built up area, but mostly, the sights were rural. They would set up their V2 – which was mobile – fire it and bugger off. So it was very difficult from our point of view. We needed a lot of luck but our philosophy was to make life as difficult as possible for the enemy and, invariably, we would do an aggressive reconnaissance over the area, and shoot anything that moved, because it would either have to be German or a collaborator. The great goal was to find a train, but we never did, because we had blown up virtually every bridge we saw. And railway embankments were good to skip with 11-second delayed-action bombs. But one of my bombs didn't delay and my poor little Spitfire had a rough ride.

602 Squadron were a great bunch of lads and we were a very tight team. But it all had to come to an end.

VE Day was amazing. We went down to the local pub and we went in our uniforms. These old guys stood up and declared, 'These are the boys that done it'. And they picked the boss and me up and put us on their shoulders and into the pub we went. Unfortunately, the ceiling in the pub was very low and we were nearly brained. I don't remember much after that!

The significance of VE Day was just out of this world.

Shortly afterwards, 602 Squadron was disbanded (19 May 1945). Shame. We were furious. And they sent ATA girls to take away our aeroplanes and we were so pissed and angry, we didn't even make a pass at them. They were lovely ladies too.

I went on leave for a while and then on 23 July, I flew to the Middle East where I converted to Mustangs.

Norman Phillips was fourteen years old at the start of the Second World War. He was evacuated to Sussex for about two years. In 1941, he started work in an office in London. He would check invoices coming though from a variety of places. He was by then in the Sea Cadets with ambitions to join the Royal Navy.

The invoices flowing through our offices were from a variety of organizations. Many of them were from local airfields and some were even from a company called BICC Cables. That company went on to be one of those involved in the manufacture of Operation Pluto (Pipe Line Under The Ocean), which was so instrumental in helping the Allied Forces fight through Europe towards the end of the war. I personally wasn't actually involved in the manufacture itself.

When I did manage to join up, I joined the Signals branch of the Royal Navy and travelled around quite a bit – Skegness, Scotland, Chatham and then the Far East. I was in that part of the world when the war ended, fighting against Japan. Consequently, VE Day had very little meaning to me personally.

On my arrival to the Far East, our first point of call was Columbo, where we were mustered for dispatch to Burma. That country had already been reclaimed from the Japanese by the time I arrived. The Royal Naval units primarily involved had been the battleship HMS *Queen Elizabeth* and the aircraft carrier HMS *Victorious*. Where I was, there was very little opposition to our arrival. The Japanese had already pulled back but we did encounter more fighting at Ramree Island.

While we were involved in supplying the 14th Army Battalion for the invasion of Rangoon, our ships were attacked from the air. Planes were diving at us, trying to get as close as possible to release their bombs. We retaliated with all guns blazing. We had heard about kamikaze pilots amongst the Japanese Air Force and were very fearful of them. After the battle, we received a note from the command, criticizing our over-indulgence and waste of ammunition. War is a strange thing.

As I said, VE Day was not really very significant for me. I was in Burma at that time, still fighting against a formidable foe. We were aware that the war in Europe had finished and did manage to squeeze in a very low key and brief celebration between bullets. Naturally, we celebrated VJ Day with more poignancy. Among other forms of celebrations, we organized a football match for the beach. It was great to be able to play sports in the open without fear of attack from the enemy.

After the war had completely finished, I became part of the occupation force in Japan. Then, I was able to see the devastation that had been raged on a defeated nation and especially the carnage and destruction caused by the atomic bombs.

Marjorie Seelig was thirty on VE Day. She was living in Bristol and had joined the ARP (Air Raid Precaution) organization. This was created before the war in anticipation of enemy attacks. She drove an ambulance but had to prepare by driving any heavy vehicle so that she could obtain her licence.

At the time, no company wanted to donate any of their best vehicles so we could only get the worst. I remember one needed a piece of string to get it started. Not many women drove vehicles at the time so quite often, people would give a double take when they saw me driving past in any old thing. When I got my heavy vehicle licence, I was put on duty in the Bristol area, and Bristol was hit very badly during the Blitz. I remember on one occasion, driving through all the bombs, when I got to the hospital, I was so nervous and shaky, the medical centre staff wasn't sure who the patient was. I'm sure that gave the patient a great deal of confidence.

I did ambulance duty until about 1941 when I decided to join the WAAF, the women's air force. That was much better because I hardly got called out at night. There was one time when we were being visited by the then Queen and during the rehearsal for the event, I got to play her.

On VE Day, I was on my way to Jerusalem. I was in a place called Gordon's Calvary. There was jubilation because we knew we would be going home.

Jean Hall was thirty-one on VE Day. She lived in Dartford, which the Luftwaffe used as one of its routes towards London.

One of the things we had on the approaches to London were large barrels filled with crude oil. On moonlit nights, when the chances of bombing attacks were greater, these barrels were set alight. The burning oil formed a smoke screen that it was hoped would keep some of the enemy pilots away. Some of these barrels were near my house. We used to see the bombers in the early morning, approaching with the sun behind them. Then we'd see the Spitfires. It was wonderful to see – scary – but wonderful. When I saw the Spitfires, I cheered and a neighbour told me off because it was all so dreadful. But I decided why shouldn't I cheer? They were our fighters attacking their bombers.

165

On one of the bombing raids, I was in hospital giving birth. All the lights went out to make it more difficult for the enemy to find anything. There were a lot of women in the ward and I remember voices calling to each other through the darkness. Then there was a scraping noise and someone decided it had to be a mouse. I just had to get out of there. I didn't like mice. With all the bombs dropping everywhere, I did not want to be in the same room as a mouse. I suppose, thinking about it now, if you worry about the little things, it helps to stop you worrying about the big things.

Dartford often got hit by bombs dropped from aircraft that were either on their way home from their targets and had not managed to drop everything beforehand, or by those that had been turned back. They weren't going to take their bombs home. It's dangerous for a plane to land with its bombs still onboard.

Towards the end of the war, the doodlebugs started falling over Dartford. On the final occasion, the house was damaged quite a lot. But it still fared better than others so we took some children in, including a baby whose mother had been killed and whose father was frantically searching. There were often a lot of people searching for others.

My husband was not called into the services because he was a manager of a company making armaments. That was his input into the war effort. In addition to that, he was also working on the anti-aircraft guns on Dartford Heath and doing fire watching in his spare time. Those guns were not really designed to hit anything. If they did, it was a bonus. They were designed more to keep enemy aircraft flying high so their aim on targets was less accurate.

I remember that one of my friends was in the RAF and was training in Canada. He was in an open cockpit plane which suddenly dropped for some reason. It left him behind, hanging in mid air and he fell onto the plane. Apparently, he landed sitting on the tail plane. I've not heard of that happening before or since.

On VE Day, I couldn't go to London as others did. So I stayed at home and spent some of the time in the church ringing the bells. I enjoyed doing that. When my husband arrived home from work, I made some sandwiches and we each loaded one of our two children on the back of a bicycle and went off into the fields where we picked bluebells. They were in season and it was such a lovely day, the weather and the realization that we weren't going to get bombed anymore.

I think the lack of interest in that time and the impact of VE Day is sad but very understandable. I was born in 1914 and wasn't particularly interested in the wars before my time, like Crimea. I can understand young people not being as interested as we are. I don't know whether it would stop another world war. I was brought up during the time after the Great War and that didn't stop another. I remember seeing an airship and I remember Armistice Day. But that's about it. So I understand the lack of interest in the Second World War. They never lived it.

Barbara Pettyfer, formerly Barbara Hussey, was twenty-one when the war finally ended. About eighteen months after the war began she and a friend realized they were very likely to be called up so they might as well volunteer. They joined the Land Army, dedicated to growing crops to feed the population. Barbara was living on the south coast and needed to be close to her mother who was ill. Sussex seemed a good choice.

My areas of work included vegetables, chickens, rabbits, fruits – that sort of thing. A woman whose brother was ill owned the area. She couldn't look after the whole market garden by herself so she contacted the Land Army to send a recruit. That was me. It was a great feeling to know you were supplying food for people who perhaps wouldn't have had it otherwise. Very little was coming in from abroad so we had to make do.

There wasn't much targeting by bombers on the fields. They were more interested in towns and factories. It was only really if the planes were on their way back home to Germany and still had a few bombs on board, they would just drop them rather than carry them back.

On one evening, I went out for a ride on my cycle and I

heard a doodlebug. I just hoped it would keep going. It didn't. It stopped. The sound of the engine stopping was really frightening. For some reason, I got off my bike and lay under a hedge. I don't know how that hedge was going to protect me. But it was just the idea of having some shelter. The bomb came down nearby. Then I got on my bike and carried on cycling home.

One of the main significances of VE Day for me was that it meant I could finally get married. I had met my future husband during the war and we decided that we would marry once the war was completely over. That, for us, was what VE Day signified. He was involved in bomb disposal so there was a lot of talk about going overseas after the war. There were a lot of bombs in Germany that had to be got rid of. And there were a lot of mines as well.

On that day, we were in Brighton. It was a little like the Trafalgar Square scene, with a huge mass of people out waving flags and celebrating. There was mass hysteria. There were flags everywhere. It was an opportunity for people to get together and celebrate.

I think that sometimes people nowadays are interested in the war, if they're in the mood for a little chat. It's like 'what did you do during the war Nan?' And then you're in. That's the opportunity to talk about it. You don't paint a pretty picture because it wasn't a pretty picture.

Alf Kennedy was twenty-six at the end of the Second World War. He served during the conflict in the Royal Engineers.

The day before I got called up, I had a narrow escape with death. I was just coming out of my flat in Bermondsey when – bang – and shrapnel flew just past my face. I actually saw it go past my nose and when it landed in the concrete, it made a hole. If I'd been just a fraction earlier, I wouldn't be talking to you now.

I did my training in Lancashire before being posted to Northern Ireland. When I went for my identity photo, I remember the officer saying to me. 'Wipe that big smile off your face. This isn't a party.' I was there when the Yanks came in towards the end of the war. I shouldn't speak out of turn about them, but I will. As an army, they left a lot to be desired – Over Sexed, Over Paid and Over Here. And the locals were something else too. When we were there first, we were treated with disdain, but when the Yanks arrived, it was like we were the locals' best friends.

The war delayed my wedding by a few days. I had planned on getting married on Christmas day but I was put on rifle practice and so the marriage had to be postponed until 4 January. I was ill just before the day but didn't say anything in case the leave was cancelled again. I got married with bombs falling all around.

I think the worst thing I ever saw in the Army wasn't actually in combat. It was on the rifle range. There was one chap who was firing dummy rounds and one exploded, blowing up the entire magazine. It took half his face off. Whenever I went to the rifle range after that, the memory was still so vivid. All I could see was this chap with half his face gone.

On VE Day, I was in Scotland, away from home but with some of my friends from the group. We had a few drinks and it was simply a case of – right now that's over, hurry up and get us home where we belong. I think I must have blown at least half of my chucking out money. I remember looking forward to going to the demob place in Guildford. I took my Army coat and flung it.

Straight away, I managed to dodge a posting to Singapore, where the Japanese were. I was so thrilled about that. For me, the war was over and that was wonderful. There was so much relief.

Neville Marshall was born in 1914. His father was a veteran of the Great War and Neville himself joined the Army and took part in the Burma campaign during the Second World War.

We started as 150 Infantry Regiment when we were sent to the Far East. That was at the beginning of the war. We were

169

ordered to Liverpool and waited there until we could get into convoy. I think we would probably have been quite a decent target for German torpedoes. On route, we stopped at Freetown where the natives greeted us by throwing oranges. Some of the troops had young children who had never seen an orange before, and here we were being bombarded by them. It was an awful waste really.

From there, we sailed to Bombay. We smelt Bombay before we reached it. The stench from the dirty water was terrible. From there, we travelled by train, in third class wooden carriages. We travelled inland for training, when we were changed from an Infantry Regiment to 150 Tank Regiment, initially without any tanks. They arrived much later.

We travelled to Burma by railway again – and guess what – third class. The Japanese occupied Burma and, once our tanks arrived, we were able to start liberating the country.

We knew nothing about what was going on at home. We were effectively cut off. My wife didn't know how I was and I didn't know how she was. She was in London, witnessing all the bombing raids.

On VE Day, I was with the rest of the guys, still fighting. You see, the war did not finish on VE Day. That was only the war in Europe. Japan was still fighting. Even VJ Day wasn't the end. Some Japanese troops continued fighting even then because they refused to believe in the concept of surrender. If you surrendered, you were inferior and they saw themselves as totally superior. I think some of them probably even refused to believe that surrender had actually taken place. The Emperor could not possibly surrender.

VE Day was being celebrated in the UK and we were still locked in battle in south-east Asia. We were still fighting and dying. VE Day made absolutely no difference. We were the Forgotten Army, left so far from home, still fighting while others enjoyed their peace.

Jack Baker was living in Oxted in Surrey when the war started and was serving in the Army by the end. He was nineteen years old on VE Day.

I had been working in a factory producing aircraft parts. I had been there for four years when, at the age of eighteen, I was called up into Army service. In 1944, I joined the 1st Battalion South Lancashire Regiment and found myself with the infantry in France.

I remember one incident in Europe so vividly. I was part of a small platoon sent to establish what was going on at the front. The Germans discovered our dug-in position and opened fire. It seemed like all hell had broken loose. To make matters worse, we were having difficulties with our Bren gun. One of my comrades – nicknamed Tojo – tried to repair the weapon and was caught in a hail of bullets. He was literally dead at the gun, with several bullets through his neck. All I had was a pistol, interestingly a Luger (what the Germans used) and a hand grenade. I was very frightened. There was a lot of shouting and a lot of crossfire before I heard what sounded like the Germans withdrawing. Minutes seemed like hours. The grenade in my hand had been relieved of the safety pin and I couldn't find it so I had to improvise. With only one free hand (the other hand holding the catch closed on the grenade) I was able to take a pin from Tojo's glasses.

When I discovered it was VE Day, I was sleeping on the floor. It was just after Bremen – our last attack. I was woken up and given a double ration of rum with the news that the war was over. I celebrated in prayer, a special comfort that has lasted for the rest of my life.

Looking back, my thoughts remain firmly with all those people who did not live to see peace. A visit to France brought it all back to me. I was surrounded by graves, tens of thousands of them. If that doesn't stop young people of today going to war, what will? In these days of a unified and friendly Europe, some people tend to wonder why we should ever go to war again. But if you can't expect individual members of families to get along with each other, how can you expect whole nations?

Evelyn Lucas was twenty-five years old at the end of the war. She joined the ATS for a bit of fun, thinking it would be far more exciting than living in a village. She hoped her involvement would take her to London. She finally achieved that ambition on VE Day.

Before I joined the ATS, my father, who was a veteran of the First World War, forbade me to join. He refused to accept that his daughter could ever contemplate volunteering to live for weeks and months on end in trenches. They were wet, boggy, smelly and a lovely haven for diseases and for rats. He often had rats running around and crawling over his feet. And of course he never knew which day would be his last. He refused to allow me to fight in the trenches because, naturally, that was his only experience of warfare.

When I did manage to join the ATS, I found myself living in a Nissan hut. As I recall, these always seemed cold, and not just in the winter. It always seemed to be colder during the war than it is now. To make matters worse, we were rarely able to light any fires.

Many of the ATS girls manned the anti-aircraft guns and I was one of the ones who was stationed in one of the gun operation rooms. From there, we used to plot the position and movement of German aircraft. The trouble was, by the time we received the information and were then able to co-ordinate it and pass it on, the enemy planes would be miles away from where they had been.

I finally got my visit to London on VE Day itself. I ventured to central London, to where the main celebrations were taking place and joined in with the festivities. It was absolutely wonderful. Everything was so tremendous. It is so difficult to describe the feeling of elation that was everywhere.

When I think about it, I doubt there will be much prospect of any celebrations these days for VE Day. The younger generation tend not to bother with things like that because they weren't directly affected. And if the young don't bother, I shouldn't think there would be much. Perhaps even politicians and the Prime Minister won't really concern themselves with it.

That's such a shame because it needs to be remembered,

even by people who have no personal experience. Perhaps there needs to be another war like that to bring back the sanity to our society.

Sheila Puckle was born a year after the Great War ended. She was related to Sir Neville Macready, the man primarily responsible for the wide scale involvement of women in warfare. When the war began, Sheila was already in the ATS, having joined the previous year.

My family had that historical link with women's warfare organizations; so joining the ATS seemed a logical step for me. I was stationed in London before the war actually started, working on anti-aircraft duties for the First Division Signals. By the outbreak of hostilities, I had transferred to Chatham.

I continued doing much the same thing as before, like many of the ATS girls did. The anti-aircraft role was a primary role for the women and, although we were not front line, we were very much in the firing line. If you can imagine, the guns and any searchlights around the vicinity, would make excellent and very visible targets for enemy aircraft and there were a lot of deaths.

Although my main base of operations was Chatham, I did find myself moving all over the country during the war. Many of the anti-aircraft guns were mobile and were shifted around the country, depending on where they were thought to be mostly needed and of course, the crews tagged along. I personally, whilst travelling around the country, had an ambition to try to get abroad.

By the end of the war, when VE Day was announced, I was in the ordnance depot in Bicester. I don't actually recall any major celebrations on that particular day. Everyone cheered, of course, but there was still plenty of work to do and every-thing just carried on as normal. It was very much business as usual. We had just experienced half a decade of war and it is impossible for an organization to simply down tools and disband in just a few hours after all that.

The bulk of any celebrations we had were reserved for the

weekend. So I suppose you could say that we didn't celebrate VE Day on VE Day, but a few days after, when there was far more opportunity. Because of organizations like us delaying the celebrations, VE Day actually lasted more than just a day.

Lena Branch was twenty-one when the war ended. She had joined the ATS in 1942 and worked mainly on an anti-aircraft gun battery in a variety of locations, depending upon where it was most urgently required. For her, the war brought with it a happy event.

I was working on 583 Mixed Heavy ack-ack battery. By mixed, I mean it was manned by men and women. We were all like one big family and there was a huge amount of respect for everyone involved. The men on the crew really respected the women.

The battery went to different locations, including New Brighton (near Liverpool), Birmingham and Seaford. Basically, we seemed to be sent anywhere that was cold and we often found ourselves perched on a cliff. When it got really cold and we had a respite from enemy attacks, we could all be seen huddled around a burner to try to keep warm.

We never shot any planes down – I don't think that was the idea. Of course, if one did come down from ground fire, then great, but the idea was to keep the planes high up so they couldn't get a proper fix on their targets. If we could manage to deter them from their targets altogether, then that was a bonus.

My main role was height finding. I used prisms to judge the height the gun needed to be at in relation to the incoming aircraft.

On one occasion, when I was home on leave, a friend of mine decided to set me up on a blind date. She may have done this for fun or trying to be nice, I'm not sure. My date was a soldier in the Royal Engineers and we became husband and wife in 1944. I remember, he was wearing his uniform on the wedding day and when he knelt at the altar, he went down on a nerve in his leg and I could hear the steady click clicking of his heels against one another. That went on until he managed to stand up. We had our honeymoon in Forest Gate, partly because it was convenient and practical and partly because we had no money. Obviously, there wasn't much opportunity for exotic overseas honeymoons in those days.

On VE Day, I was at home. I had by then left the ATS with a surprise package – a daughter – and she really was a surprise. Although the ATS had been a wonderful and friendly organization, I was glad to be where I was, living with my mum in Maidstone. I remember there not being much need for shelters there for some reason. Obviously, Maidstone had not been a prime target and by the end of the war, the small number of shelters there had been was on a rapid decline.

We were living on an estate where everybody knew everybody else. The companionship was terrific during those earlier years and I think we had demonstrated to the world that we were very resourceful and resilient, more so than people tend to be these days. We were able to hold a terrific street party at the end and I remember someone playing an accordion. I also know that, unlike a scene of today, there was one solitary car parked on the entire street.

I was thrilled about the prospect of VE Day for a number of reasons. It meant I could raise my child in the comparative safety of post war Europe without too much fear of bombing raids and having to go away for weeks at a time to shoot at enemy planes. It also meant that the country could be lit again. Lights were on everywhere. That signalled the end of the regular blackouts we had endured for so long as an attempt to prevent the German pilots finding attractive targets for their bombs and bullets. I think it is poignant to point out that, at the time, although everything was so dark at night, it was far safer to walk around in the dark then than it is now. The danger then had come from above, not like the danger now that comes from behind.

After sixty years since VE Day, I feel that the young of today seem to have no real respect for anyone. Some do – don't get me wrong. But so many seem to have lost that quality along the way. Sixty years is a long time for society to change. So few even give the struggles of the war a moment's thought unless they are told about it and, even then they do not really understand. At the time of the war, we rarely thought of the danger. We just got on with the job. I wonder whether people in future years will have that kind of resilience, if indeed it's ever needed.

George Phillips was serving in the Home Guard during some of the war years, before volunteering to join the Royal Navy at the age of seventeen. He was twenty-one when the war ended.

I was serving on minesweepers, primarily HMS *Espiegle*. We were part of the Glorious Twelfth, a flotilla that had destroyed more mines than any other Royal Naval minesweeper flotilla. Our main areas of operation were the Adriatic, the Mediterranean and the Aegean. As well as minesweeping, we were also involved in submarine hunting and carried depth charges.

Like so many other flotillas, we suffered casualties. An Italian submarine sank our leader. The disaster became worse than even that. The depth charges the sweeper carried, which had been primed ready for use, exploded on contact with the water. So much for the shilling per day danger pay.

About fourteen months before D-Day, we assisted in the campaign to take Sicily. Malta, being nearby and under Allied control, was used as a base from which the operation was mounted. But the largest hurdle was when we were involved in the mine clearance operation for the taking of Greece. By the end, we had received medals from Malta, Anzio and Greece. But we were just doing our jobs; we were doing what was required of us.

On VE Day, I was working, doing the same as I had been doing. I was aboard the minesweeper, clearing mines off the coast of Northern Italy. In addition to the usual methods of locating mines, we were also by then using information from captured enemy maps and from aircraft flypasts. The actual impact of what VE Day meant for so many people did not really sink in for me – there was still so much work to do. The seaways were still a very unsafe place to be and that had to be rectified as safely and swiftly as possible. I was keen to return home though. I had a girlfriend waiting for me and did manage to get home for two weeks leave just before Christmas 1945. But otherwise, it was business as usual. The only difference after the end of the war was that we didn't have the added dangers of submarine, ship or air attack to complicate the mine clearance work.

One of the biggest differences between how we lived then and how people of the same age live now is the lack of discipline in modern life. I really don't feel we would ever be able to fight another war in a similar vein, if it ever became necessary. No one would be able to cope with situations like rationing. People would simply smash windows and grab what they could so they had a bit more than everyone else.

Helen Carter was twenty on VE Day. She was living in Hampstead in London when war broke out and then served in the Women's Royal Naval Service from 1942 to 1946.

The day war broke out, we heard our first air raid siren. With my family, I went out onto the balcony of the flat to see if we could witness anything. I'm not quite sure what we expected to see – bombs falling all around us maybe? Very soon, everyone in the entire block pitched in to build an air raid shelter beneath the building. It was here that we would all find ourselves during air raids.

On one occasion, a really unusual incident occurred. We had a close encounter with a bomb. Not unusual itself at that time, but the result certainly was. The explosion ripped our back door away, yet a window beside it did not even suffer a single crack.

I don't think rationing had a devastating affect on us as a family. We were all great vegetable eaters and vegetables were reasonably plentiful. That stated, the ration on sweets did affect me.

When the war finally ended, I was in London. My boyfriend at the time was Chilean and I was spending the day with him at South America House. This was a place where South American volunteers could stay whilst on leave. In the evening, we made our way towards Buckingham Palace. It took a long time to get there, in fact an inordinate length of time. What delayed us were quite simply the crowds. Seemingly everyone we encountered wanted us to join them for a drink and a dance. The atmosphere was absolutely intoxicating, even without too much drink.

I don't recall seeing Winston Churchill on the balcony at Buckingham Palace, but I certainly do recall seeing the Royal Family. I'm sure they appeared several times. When I turned around on one occasion, I was thrilled to see J. B. Priestley behind me.

The previous major anniversary of VE Day – the fiftieth – was extremely significant for me. But there are now so many people who know nothing about the war and all it meant that I think the interest has dropped. Most people don't seem all that interested and I think it should perhaps all be gently allowed to fade.

Margaret Smith was twenty-one at the end of the war in Europe. She recalls how she felt that the war years had become a real step forwards for women and a real eye-opening experience for her. As soon as she had the opportunity, she joined the Women's Royal Naval Service.

I was at school when the war started. I was living in a large rented house in Bedford and we had a large number of evacuees billeted with us. There were also some soldiers there too, some of the ones who had returned from the evacuation at Dunkirk. I remember my mother insisting that the soldiers have their shirts washed before they did anything else. When there was a row of shirts hanging on the line, a corporal arrived at the door and informed the soldiers they all had to report to the market square. We had great fun trying to get the shirts dry in time, resorting to using electric fires. The soldiers had to go off to the square literally steaming.

Rationing, we found, affected everyone to some degree,

and often animals too. Our neighbour was a conductor. His dog managed to gain access somehow to our meat store and stole a shoulder of lamb. We were extremely annoyed about that because we had saved up quite a few of our coupons to get it. And there it was – gone.

After joining up, I was posted to Windsor and worked as a pay writer for merchant shipping. But I very rarely actually saw a sailor. I was working with an ex-chief stoker whose jokes I learnt to laugh at, even if I didn't understand them. I will always remember having to march to Windsor Castle and seeing the then Princess Elizabeth in her uniform.

On VE Day, I decided to walk to Windsor. I had arranged to meet up with some schoolboys from Eton and we did the conga dance along the high street at Eton. That was really about it. That was how I celebrated the day and now, after all these years, I think there is still plenty of attention and thought given to VE Day. But I would like to see more done about VJ Day. After the original VJ Day, I was posted to India and the Far East, where I encountered some of the ex-prisoners of war from Burma. Their general condition was very upsetting.

Margaret Harris was twenty-seven years old when the war against Germany ended. She served in the Women's Royal Naval Service, although, as she recalls, it had taken a while to get involved. Like so many others, she told of a VE Day filled with very little celebration. It was more a case of business as usual.

When war broke out, I was living at home in Scotland. I was living with my father in a large Victorian house that had been built by my great-uncle in 1884. Since we had spare accommodation, we were obliged to take in some evacuees. We received a mother and six children from Glasgow. They missed the city life and as soon as there was an opportunity, they returned. They had only been with us for about three or four months. It is nice that they continued to remain in contact for many years after.

I had applied to join the WRNS and at first, heard nothing.

I had to make several enquiries and it was 1940 by the time I was asked to attend an interview in Glasgow and later that year before I entered service. I found myself working in a bedroom in a station hotel.

I really enjoyed my time in the service and met many interesting people. Because of my secretarial experience, I started as a writer. But I managed to place myself on an officer training course in Greenwich. Once that had finished, I became a cipher officer.

I found this very interesting although sometimes it was confusing isolating all the information I had and remembering whether I had seen or heard something in the news or in a message at work. All the big items, like Churchill's meetings and the campaigns could only be 'unbuttoned' by the head of the watch. There was always a huge flow of paperwork. Greenock, where I was stationed, had the largest flow of naval signals outside the Admiralty in London.

I made trips across the Atlantic during the war and it was whilst I was returning from America that I heard the news that Germany had surrendered. Yet even despite that, we still had to alter course to avoid a U-boat. 'Don't they know the war's over?' I found myself wondering. Because of the dodging of U-boats and the consequent altering of our course, by the time we arrived back into base, it was all over. Greenock had finished the celebrations. The troopship I was on was even 'dry'. So much for that. We missed the celebrations because it was business as usual.

Chapter Twenty-One

The Media and VE Day

While compiling this book many original documents were collected, including original newspapers and magazines showcasing VE Day.

In the UK, paper was a precious commodity during the Second World War so the daily newspapers were not very thick. The *Daily Mail* on 8 May 1945, for example, had just eight pages but it tells us much about the social history of its day.

Of particular note is the euphoria of the day itself as far as homegrown celebration is concerned. Underneath the headline 'VE-Day! It's Over in the West', is the announcement of a 'War Winners' radio broadcast from the BBC in the evening which would begin with an address by the Archbishop of Canterbury followed by a service of thanksgiving. The King would then speak to the nation after which there would be speeches from Field Marshal Montgomery, Field Marshal Alexander and General Eisenhower, whose contributions had been recorded. The entire programme was scheduled to last for seven hours.

With the paper going to press in the early hours of 'VE-Eve' there was still much to report, as another journalist announced whilst standing in Piccadilly Circus. His first words were: 'This is it – and we are all going nuts!' and continued by reporting that there were countless people but the police estimate was 10,000. He, however, believed that to be a conservative estimate. The feature continues on the back page with a large photograph.

A smaller story announced the victory celebrations in

Washington and New York, which included a report of a 'continuous' shower of paper falling from skyscrapers and radio announcers pleading 'Don't throw paper; it's necessary to the war.' There was an even shorter piece announcing that the war with Japan was still ongoing. A minor point amidst all the celebrations it seemed!

Most interesting are the cartoons, with Popeye on the 'Good Ship Freedom' beating up a Nazi; whilst 'Jane' announced that she would soon be out of her uniform, whereupon seven men ripped her clothes off declaring that she had just been demobbed.

The *Daily Mirror* was full of quips and reports of the celebrations with the exception of page 2, which stated that there <u>was</u> still a war to be won, with virtually the whole page dedicated to a large cartoon of a heavily bandaged soldier offering a wreath with a card that stated 'Victory and peace in Europe'. The caption just below a scene of dead bodies draped over demolished buildings read: 'Here you are – don't lose it again'.

The letters page was, as ever in historical papers, of much interest. There was a headline letter from an ex-serviceman trying to find work but nobody wanted him; then there was the humour of a lady who wished to share a joke about a greengrocer who was offering potatoes for 4d a pound, but only to those people who bought them the previous week for 8s a pound. There was hope, thanks and an undertone of heavy relief throughout, which echoes the recollections in this book.

However if one is looking for interesting, factual anecdotes, one must look to page 7. One such interesting piece concerned an RAF officer's wife who was acquitted on a charge of murdering her husband (a squadron leader) and had collapsed in the dock. A letter found on the dead man implied that he was having an affair. The defence was that the husband came home, threatened to murder his wife, but in the ensuing struggle a revolver went off.

An historic but tiny news item announced the commencement of professional football in England and Wales, stating that the first and second divisions would be split into North and South and both halves of the third division would follow suit.

Horse racing had resumed for 'Victory Week' but whether there were still celebrations at the winning post is anybody's guess!

The *Daily Mirror* featured a short but mixed bag of stories – both funny and sad. However, if we look back at the *Sunday Express* on 6 May, the end of the war had a slightly different complexion. The articles were more newsy and hard hitting, simply because the war wasn't officially over then. The *Sunday Express* adopted a 'breaking news' philosophy to the whole issue which was, no doubt, both informative and thought provoking. It asked the question 'How are we going to clean this lot up now?'

One of the lead stories concerned the US and British breakdown of communication with Russia over the future of Poland. Germans in Norway 'offer to give in' and the Desert Rats took a headline as they went into Denmark. The *Sunday Express* must have made exciting reading for its 2 million readers, especially tiny one paragraph snippets, such as the news that Hitler's chalet at Berchtesgaden was on fire. One thought-provoking item concerned the on-going search for an eight month old baby snatched from his pram in Oxford Street on 16 April while his mother was shopping. The baby was the son of a Polish soldier.

Canada had reputedly offered their condolences to the German minister in Dublin for the death of Hitler, with a paragraph stating that films or newsreels showing victims of concentration camps would not be shown in Eire.

There was an announcement by the Ministry of Fuel and Power that coal supplies would be restricted until the end of April 1946. This again clearly shows that hardships continued after the war; indeed rationing would continue until the 1950s. However, there was also an interesting piece on how to grow mushrooms in your air raid shelter after the war!

The letters page was concerned with the restoration of people's right to work, a quandary many people found themselves in – being selected for a job but having the Ministry of Labour blocking the decision.

The entertainment section offered a diverse selection of films including George Sanders in Oscar Wilde's *Picture of Dorian Gray* and Abbott and Costello in *Here Come the Co-eds*.

The football highlights recorded that Manchester United drew 1-1 with Chesterfield, Fulham beat Charlton 5-3 and Wales lost 3-2 to England.

A popular American news magazine – then as now – was *Time* and the issue for the week commencing 14 May 1945 celebrated Victory in Europe with an appropriate cover: an American, a British and a Russian soldier (in that order) standing shoulder-to-shoulder and waving their respective flags.

Inside was a mixture of features. One of the most interesting (under the heading of 'Medicine') concerned living victims of concentration camps and how they were now going to be treated. There were several photos from concentration camps, really hitting the latest news from Europe home to the Americans. A seven page feature entitled 'Victory in Europe' culminated with the sub-feature 'US at War'. They were quite interesting from a British point of view, as they clearly showed America's efforts and show-cased their triumphs and tribulations. One of the readers' letters claimed that the war began with the bombing of Pearl Harbor!

In spite of the euphoria and the celebrations of VE Day the newspapers, both British and American, showed simply that life went on. Europe needed rebuilding and there was still war with Japan.

The media were happy to celebrate in the most appropriate way for their readers, but at the same time, there was a genuine feeling of sobriety.

Conclusion

Moving On

During the writing of this book some of the contributors have sadly died. Thankfully, we have a snap-shot of their memories here; something to ponder and, hopefully, learn from.

VE Day was more than a street party; it was a signal to those who still struggled, that good was finally transcending evil. It is right that we mark the anniversary of such a significant day as VE Day. Sixty years isn't such a long time. People still remember the difficulties, the sacrifices, the need and they will continue to do so. But, as the years pass, there will be fewer people to contribute to such a book as this. John Campbell was one who did contribute. He said:

> I think there is not much emphasis placed on VE Day now, except by ex-servicemen. They lost friends. In the services, we were all friends and to lose someone was always hard to accept, although I knew there was a chance it could happen. There was great comradeship. I have met quite a few of the younger generation who, whilst they have no memory of the war, do give me a lot of respect, especially when I'm on parade. They sometimes come up to me and ask me what I know and I tell them. They are often quite interested.

So let this book, with the varied memories of the people who were there, be a reminder of the end of the Second World War and the defeat of Hitler and Nazism, and a reference for those who are interested in what happened sixty years ago.

These stories are the stories of ordinary people; people who denounced Hitler and all his works; people who fought for what they thought was right.

Thankfully, there are still good people today who are willing to do that.

Appendix A

How to Surrender

Just before the formal surrenders, millions of leaflets were dropped over Germany. It was intended to explain how to correctly declare an intention to surrender, giving the proper pronunciation. Although it was specifically targeted at German troops, there was nothing stopping civilians using it. Here it is reproduced as it originally read, with an English translation.

Ei Ssorrender
  Dies ist die englische und amerikanische Aussprache des Wortes "I surrender" (Ich orgebe mich). Macht davon Gebrauch, wem sich Gelegenheit ergibt.

I Surrender
  This is the English and American pronunciation of the words "I Surrender". Make use of it, if you have the opportunity.

Appendix B

Victory In Europe Speeches

General Eisenhower
Supreme Commander, Allied Expeditionary Force,
7 May 1945

In January 1943, the late President Roosevelt and Premier Churchill met in Casablanca. There, they pronounced the formula of unconditional surrender for the Axis Powers. In Europe, that formula has now been fulfilled. The Allied Force, which invaded Europe on June 6, 1944, has, with its great Russian ally, and forces advancing in the south, utterly defeated the Germans by land, sea and air. Thus, unconditional surrender has been achieved by teamwork, teamwork not only among all the Allies participating but amongst all the services – land, sea and air. To every subordinate that has been in this command, of almost 5,000,000 Allies, I owe a debt of gratitude that can never be repaid. The only repayment that can be made to them is the deep appreciation and lasting gratitude of all free citizens of all the United Nations.

Count Schwerin von Krasigk,
Reich Foreign Minister.
7 May 1945

German men and women. The German High Command has today, on the order of Grand Admiral Dönitz, announced the unconditional surrender of all fighting troops. After almost six years of heroic struggle and unequalled severity, the strength of Germany has succumbed to the overwhelming might of our enemies. The continuation of the war would mean only senseless bloodshed and useless devastation.

No one should be deceived as to the severity of the conditions which our enemies will impose on the German people. We must face them squarely and soberly, without questioning. No one can doubt that the coming period will be hard for each one of us and will demand sacrifices in all walks of life . . . We can only hope that the atmosphere of hatred which today surrounds Germany in the eyes of the world will make way for a spirit of conciliation among the nations, without which the recovery of the world is impossible.

Field Marshal Montgomery
Commander In Chief, 21 British Army Group
8 May 1945

What I have to say is very simple and quite short. I would ask you all to remember those of our comrades who fell in this struggle. They gave their lives that others might have freedom, and no man can do more than that. I believe that He would say to each one of them: 'Well done, thou good and faithful servant' . . . We must remember to give praise and thankfulness where it is due. This is the Lord's doing, and it is marvellous in our eyes . . .

Few commanders can have had such loyal service as you have given me. I thank each one of you from the bottom of my heart . . . We have won the German War; now let us win the peace. Good luck to you all, wherever you may be.

Air Chief Marshal Sir Arthur Tedder
Deputy Supreme Commander, Allied Expeditionary Force
8 May 1945

This has been every man's and every woman's war. Regardless of uniform, rank or race, the men and women of the United Nations have each made their own contribution in blood and sweat to victory. Today is their day . . . your day. Well done, every one of you.

Appendix C

Allied Casualties from D-Day
to VE Day

(Not including any losses incurred by the Soviet Union, those held
in prisoner of war camps or concentration camps, Allied troops
lost fighting against Japan, and civilian casualties.)

	Killed or died of wounds	*Wounded*	*Missing or captured*	*Total*
British	30,276	96,672	14,698	141,646
Canadian	10,739	30,906	2,247	43,892
American	109,824	356,661	56,632	523,117
French	12,587	49,513	4,726	66,826
Other Allies	1,528	5,011	354	6,893
Total	164,954	538,763	78,657	782,374

Bibliography

Gilbert, Martin, *Second World War*, Fontana, 1990.
—— *The Day The War Ended*, HarperCollins, 1996.
Hollister, Paul (ed), *From D-Day Through Victory In Europe*, Columbia Broadcasting System (CBS), 1945.
Kecskemeti, Paul, *Strategic Surrender*, Stanford University Press, 1978.
Longmate, Norman, *When We Won The War*, Hutchinson & Co. Ltd., 1977.
Mantale, Ivor, *World War II – 50th Anniversary of Victory in World War II*, CLB Publishing, nd.
Miller, Russell, *Ten Days In May*, Michael Joseph Ltd., 1995.